Alice Beile-Bowes und Werner Beile

Kommentierte Übersetzungstexte für Fortgeschrittene

Deutsch – Englisch

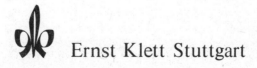

Alice Beile-Bowes, M. A., Lehrbeauftragte, und
Werner Beile, Lektor,
am Englischen Seminar der Ruhr-Universität, Bochum

Quellennachweis

Verlag Ludwig Auer, Donauwörth (Text 4); August Bagel Verlag, Düsseldorf (Text 14); Ernst Klett Verlag, Stuttgart (Texte 3, 8, 12); VEB Max Niemeyer Verlag, Halle/Leipzig (Text 6); Georg Picht, Hinterzarten (Text 5); Hans Sahl, New York (Text 13); Verlag G. Schulte-Bulmke, Frankfurt am Main (Text 7); Der Spiegel (Texte 9, 10); Verlag Vandenhoeck & Ruprecht, Göttingen (Text 1); Die Zeit (Texte 2, 11)

1. Auflage   1 4 3 2 1 | 1978 77 76 75

Alle Drucke dieser Auflage können im Unterricht nebeneinander benutzt werden. Die letzte Zahl bezeichnet das Jahr dieses Druckes.
© Ernst Klett Verlag, Stuttgart 1975. Nach dem Urheberrechtsgesetz vom 9. Sept. 1965 i. d. F. vom 10. Nov. 1972 ist die Vervielfältigung oder Übertragung urheberrechtlich geschützter Werke, also auch der Texte, Illustrationen und Graphiken dieses Buches, nicht gestattet. Dieses Verbot erstreckt sich auch auf die Vervielfältigung für Zwecke der Unterrichtsgestaltung – mit Ausnahme der in den §§ 53, 54 URG ausdrücklich genannten Sonderfälle –, wenn nicht die Einwilligung des Verlages vorher eingeholt wurde. Im Einzelfall muß über die Zahlung einer Gebühr für die Nutzung fremden geistigen Eigentums entschieden werden. Als Vervielfältigung gelten alle Verfahren einschließlich der Fotokopie, der Übertragung auf Matrizen, der Speicherung auf Bändern, Platten, Transparenten oder anderen Medien.
Druck: Druckerei A. Röhm, 7032 Sindelfingen, Böblinger Straße 68
ISBN: 3-12-510200-6

Inhalt

Introduction 5

1. Aldous Huxley 12
2. Treibhaus der Traditionen 18
3. Der Film im Fremdsprachenunterricht 26
4. Über den Lernprozeß 30
5. Die deutsche Bildungskatastrophe 34
6. Die Entstehung des Romans 40
7. Die Bedeutung des autobiographischen Schrifttums 44
8. Analyse eines *comic strip* auf der Oberstufe 50
9. Ein Sowjet-Journalist über den amerikanischen Lebensstil (1) 56
10. Ein Sowjet-Journalist über den amerikanischen Lebensstil (2) 62
11. Fragen der Sozialpolitik 66
12. Texte im Anfangsunterricht 72
13. Über die 20er Jahre 80
14. Aus dem Vorwort zu einer Interpretationssammlung 84

Wichtige Hilfsmittel 91
Index 95

Introduction

The general aim of this book of translation texts and commentaries is to provide a means of individual practice for the advanced student of English to improve his understanding and production of the written English of formal exposition. The target population, then, is students of English in universities and colleges of education.

Origin of texts and commentaries

These commentaries are the result of work in translation classes in the Englisches Seminar of the Ruhr-Universität Bochum carried out by the authors — a German and an English native speaker respectively. The texts to be translated are of contemporary German, from books, articles and newspapers, and chosen from the fields of general education, language teaching methodology, literary criticism, and cultural background information, as these were areas in which the students were already familiar with English texts as part of their studies, and where any subject-specific vocabulary would either be known to them, or if not known, could usefully be learnt.

The selection of items included in the commentary to each text, and the remarks to each of them, were initially based on an informal analysis of students' written translations, between 30 and 60 for each text. A detailed list of errors and variants was drawn up and a first commentary prepared for use with the original group of students, when their work was returned and discussed in class. The same texts were used again with other groups of students this time orally in class, to check the validity of the list of errors and variants, and also the usefulness of the comments for the students. The choice of items, then, and the comments on them, were not made arbitrarily, from the point of view of the teacher/author, but as a result of experience with successive classes of students, from the point of view of the learner.

The validity of the translations and commentaries from the point of view of acceptability was checked by a group of British 'Lektoren' in the English Department of this university.

The comments fall roughly into four broad categories:

1. the indication of frequent sources of error together with a justification of the version suggested and an explanation of why certain versions are unacceptable,

2. the indication of acceptable alternative syntactic patterns and lexical items,
3. the treatment of certain areas of lexis from the point of view of appropriateness, collocation, congruence, etc.,
4. the indication of certain problems arising from the very nature of translation — what to take into account when rendering metaphors, the choice between a lengthy but exact paraphrase and a near-synonym, intranslatability, etc.

Translation in foreign-language-teaching

The word translation in a foreign-language-teaching context is weighed down by negative connotations with the grammar-translation method, yet a rejection of the grammar-translation method does not necessarily involve the rejection of all forms of grammar teaching, or of translation as one exercise-form among many. The possibilities of translation as an exercise-form, albeit with limited, newly-formulated aims, and particularly with advanced students, remain to be explored in a less prejudiced light.

The adherents of a strictly monolingual approach reject translation as being an interlingual process, and fail to see that while non-dogmatic monolingualism continues to be valid as a principle for the main part of language-teaching, particularly in the acquisition years, the interlingual situation is probably just as frequent in real life as the monolingual situation — for example, the German talking to English friends in Germany and possibly translating for them, the German group (of school-children, of friends, of businessmen) talking German to each other and English to their hosts, the German writing letters in English on behalf of German friends, or vice versa. There is a moral in the (true) tale of the German student who, after nine years of strict monolingual teaching, when faced with an English newspaper text and asked for a comment in German, became totally inarticulate, and then confessed in English, "I know what it means, but I can't say it in German".

The followers of a strictly skill-orientated approach to foreign-language-teaching argue that translating can teach nothing but the skill of translating, a skill which only needs to be mastered by future translators. However they do not apply the same criteria to other exercise-forms, but postulate a certain 'transferability' of part-skills and knowledge learned. They expect a language laboratory drill to teach more than simply how to do a language laboratory drill, and they expect the construction of a dialogue in the classroom to lead to more than the ability to construct dialogues in the classroom. An exercise-form is selected for use according to whether the functions it fulfils are suitable to a certain teaching aim. Similarly, the grounds for rejecting an exercise-form can only be that the functions it fulfils are unsuited to the teaching aim. The total rejection of an exercise-form which is not based on an examination of its functions is not admissible.

In translating, the student is practising the precise reproduction of a given content (which he receives as a text in the expression form of his native language) in the expression form of the target language. Here we are training his ability to express himself in the target language as correctly as possible as regards form and as precisely as possible as regards meaning. This type of practice is not possible, for example, in the essay, where the student is not bound to the expressing of a precise content, and where it is therefore impossible to control how precisely what he writes corresponds with what he intends to say or even if he is aware of the precise meaning of what he writes. The translation might be seen as a preliminary step to the essay, and could in practice be closely linked to it.

In the attempt to find English equivalents as exact in meaning as the original German the student is forced to consider consciously and intensively the precise meaning of the means of expression at his disposal. Doing this in a controlled situation will reveal to him where exact meanings are not in fact understood, where there are gaps in his knowledge. This in turn should enable him consciously and systematically to correct and extend his repertoire in the foreign language. Thus the student gains more control over the language at his disposal, more insight into his own needs and more control over his own individual learning process. Further, the confrontation of the two languages helps him to understand problems of interference in preparation for his future role as a teacher of English.

Translation is only one of a whole range of interlingual reproduction activities which all prepare the learner, particularly the advanced learner, for his possible role as intermediary between other English and German speakers.

Aim of the material

The aim of this particular collection was to provide practice material which would give the student the sort of information he needs and seeks in order to improve his own performance in the written language and extend his knowledge of English. Further that it should also be effective in that by giving the student insight into the points dealt with it enables him to learn cognitively. The student should have the means of studying questions of syntax and vocabulary, of synonymy, style, register, appropriateness, etc., with concrete examples, and also in context. He should also have a means of measuring his own performance against a standard.

Collections of texts with possible translations and brief sets of footnotes have proved to be of restricted use, and ineffective in their method of teaching; of restricted use, since lack of space makes it impossible to answer the students' most frequent questions — why certain versions are preferable to others and why certain versions are unacceptable; ineffective, because the student can only learn by the mechanical memorizing of scanty information on a right/wrong basis, having no opportunity to learn cognitively by insight into the problem.

The commentaries are by no means exhaustive in the sense that all the questions a student could conceivably have are dealt with, neither are they exhaustive in the sense that there is nothing more to say on the points dealt with. The commentaries, however, answer the majority of the questions which, according to our experience with these texts, students are likely to have.

Translation, interpretation and subjectivity

Every translation involves an interpretation of the original text, and this interpretation is necessarily subjective. Where students disagreed among each other as to the correct interpretation of the German text, we have indicated this in the commentary, and offered alternative translations. The choice of adequate English equivalents is also necessarily subjective. We have tried to reduce this subjectivity on our part by validation of the English version and the commentary with a group of English native speakers, all with a good knowledge of German.

The translations are not to be regarded as 'best versions', indeed, no two native speakers would ever agree on the same 'best' version of a longer translation text; rather, they are to be regarded as sample versions, and, particularly, versions which are within the scope of the student. Many possible lexical and syntactic variants which would have been equally acceptable have been indicated. Here, again, it was not possible to be exhaustive, but we hope that we have indicated a sufficiently large number of variants to cover the queries of most students.

However much the translator tries to reduce subjectivity in his interpretation of the source text and in his selection of equivalents for his translation, a certain degree of subjectivity must remain. Where problems of translation arose which really did involve a question of personal preference on our part, the reasons for the final choice are given. Particularly these comments may be of interest to those concerned not with translation as an exercise-form but with the science of translating, as they reveal the considerations the translator has taken into account together with the concrete example. A criticism of the translations then, must take into account the reasons given for the choice of translation, and the specific aim of these translations, orientated as they are towards language-teaching.

The sample translation offers a contextual framework within which elements can be replaced, and against which elements can be measured.

The introduction to a collection of teaching-materials based on the translation as an exercise-form cannot be the place to deal at length with the science of translating and the many unanswered problems involved, such as hypotheses about the way in which the message is transferred from the source language to the target language. The important issue is the examination of the adequacy, appropriateness, etc. of the translation product, i.e. the use of contrastive techniques in one aspect of language-teaching. Thus the emphasis lies on the product of translation rather than the process. Here we would refer the reader to the publications, including bibliographies, listed at the end of this book for a more detailed treatment of this field.

Method of procedure

The following order of progress has proved the most effective method of working with this book.

1. Translation (phase of familiarization with the problems involved)

The student prepares a translation of the text, either as a whole, or in sections, consulting grammars and dictionaries as he wishes, but without consulting the sample translation and commentary. This phase of intensive work on the text is the necessary preliminary to drawing full benefit from the commentary.

2. Comparison with sample text and commentary (phase of cognition)

Being thoroughly familiar with the text and its problems, the student is now in a position to absorb and reflect on the information given in the sample text and commentary, and modify his version accordingly. If the first phase is omitted, the information offered in the second phase is probably too concentrated to be absorbed completely, with the result that it is only partially retained, and the work is thus ineffective.

3. Re-translation (phase of consolidation)

Ideally, having worked through the commentary, the student re-translates the text, correcting his mistakes and improving his translation. This is the phase of consolidation, in which the student recycles the information he has received in the second phase. This third phase is probably as necessary to a retention of the information offered as is the first phase.

Additional remarks

The following works are indicated by the abbreviated references in the commentaries to more detailed treatment of the point under discussion:

Friederich	=	W. Friederich: *Technik des Übersetzens: Englisch und Deutsch.* München 1969.
Leech	=	G. N. Leech: *Meaning and the English Verb.* London 1971.
Quirk et al.	=	R. Quirk, S. Greenbaum, G. Leech, J. Svartvik: *A Grammar of Contemporary English.* London 1972.
SOED	=	*The Shorter Oxford English Dictionary on Historical Principles.* Prepared by W. Little, H. W. Fowler, J. Coulson. Revised and edited by C. T. Onions. Third Edition. Oxford 1965 (1944).

A list of further works of reference is given at the end of the book. The student should familiarize himself with these works.

In addition, an alphabetical register of the grammatical items dealt with in this book as well as those of the lexical items which we consider to be of sufficiently general interest has been included for the convenience of the student, so that these materials can also be used as a source of reference for the treatment of language problems in context.

A collection of texts for translation in class (*Gestufte Übersetzungstexte für Fortgeschrittene*, Klettbuch 5101, herausgegeben von Werner Beile und Dieter Hamblock) graded according to level of difficulty and subject matter is available parallel to this book. Students using it might find it helpful to study authentic English texts on the same or similar topics before attempting a translation.

The commentary refers to the English text. The items are presented in chronological order as they occur in the English text, the number referring to the line in which they occur. For ease of reference, each comment is headed not only by the item from the English text but also by the part of the German text the meaning of which it renders. It must be stressed that these two items do not have the function of dictionary equivalents, but are to be seen as equivalents *in the appropriate context.* Thus they may occupy syntactically quite different positions in the English and German sentences. The form given is that which appears in the text, not necessarily the basic form.

An asterisk (*) preceding an item indicates that it is unacceptable.

When words are not used in their normal communicative function, i. e. when reference is made to an item as a form rather than a meaning, the words are printed in italics. An item in single inverted commas indicates a meaning rather than a form.

In conclusion we should like to thank Mr M. Bacon, BA, Mr D. Bonnyman, MA, BPhil, and Mr R. W. O. Drysdale, MA, for their helpful comments, and the many students, who through their cooperation made it possible for us to hand down their experience to successive generations of students.

Ruhr-Universität   Alice Beile-Bowes
Bochum 1974   Werner Beile

1. Aldous Huxley

Wenn wir den psychologischen Roman als einen der wesentlichen Beiträge unseres Jahrhunderts zur abendländischen Literatur betrachten, gebührt dem 1965 verstorbenen Huxley ein Ehrenplatz unter seinen Vertretern. Sein Blick dringt tief in die Psyche des modernen Menschen ein, und mit einem harten, spitzen Stift hält er den Befund fest. Er hat zwar trotz des vernunftmäßig konzipierten Überbaus, der seine bedeutendsten Werke kennzeichnet, keine neuen Formen geschaffen wie James, Conrad, Joyce, D. Richardson und V. Woolf – im Gegenteil: seine Romane weisen die lockere Struktur der Werke von Butler und Wells auf, und wie diese bieten sie die Theorie oft in einer kaum objektivierten, essayhaften Form. Er hat den „inneren Monolog" nicht verwendet, und er bemüht sich auch nicht um die Austilgung der Spuren des künstlerischen Ich. Hierin gleicht er D. H. Lawrence, mit dem ihn eine lebenslängliche Freundschaft verband, und wie dieser ist er tief beunruhigt über die Situation des Menschen in unserem technischen, zerebralen Zeitalter. Auch er erkennt die größte Gefahr für diesen in dem Sich-Abfinden mit seiner Umwelt. Herkunft und Persönlichkeit ließen ihn jedoch andere Wege als Lawrence einschlagen, um das Dilemma zu überwinden; er propagiert nicht die Besinnung auf die totale menschliche Natur und eine entsprechende Lebensweise, sondern ihm geht es um die Rettung des geistigen Menschen, und immer mehr konzentrierte er seine Aufmerksamkeit auf die religiösen Bedürfnisse, die unter den heutigen Voraussetzungen entweder verkümmern oder in Ideologien ihre trügerische Befriedigung finden. Von den meisten anderen Dichtern, die ein ähnliches Anliegen ausdrücken – wie T. S. Eliot, G. Greene, E. Waugh –, unterscheidet sich Huxley dadurch, daß er die Lösung des Problems nicht im Bekenntnis zu einer der bestehenden kollektiven Glaubensformen sieht, sondern er sucht als erlebendes Individuum den Zugang zum Göttlichen außerhalb der Dogmen und erkennt ihn in einer Synthese dessen, was allen großen Religionen gemein ist.

Aus: R. Fricker, *Der moderne englische Roman.* 2. Aufl., Göttingen: Vandenhoeck & Ruprecht, 1966.

Commentary

1 **if** – wenn: if *wenn* bears the meaning of 'jedesmal wenn', then it expresses the meaning conveyed by *when/whenever*. If on the other hand the clause

1. Aldous Huxley

If we regard the psychological novel as one of the most significant contributions of our century to Western literature, then Huxley, who died in 1965, deserves a place of honour among its exponents. His gaze penetrates deep into the psyche of modern man and he sets down what he finds with a
5 hard, sharp pen. In spite of the rationally conceived structure that characterizes his most important works, he failed to create new forms as James, Conrad, Joyce, D. Richardson and V. Woolf did — on the contrary, his novels reveal the loose structure of the works of Butler and Wells, and as in these, theory is often presented in an essay-like form that could hardly be
10 called objective. He did not employ interior monologue, nor did he seek to eradicate all traces of the presence of the author. In this respect he resembles D. H. Lawrence, his lifelong friend, and like him he is deeply disturbed about the situation of man in our technical cerebral age. He, too, sees man's greatest danger in his resigned acceptance of his environment. His upbringing and his
15 personality made him take other paths than Lawrence to overcome the dilemma. He does not propagate the contemplation of human nature in its entirety, and a corresponding way of life; rather, he is concerned with saving spiritual man, and he concentrates his attention more and more on the religious needs that in present-day conditions either wither away or find their
20 deceptive satisfaction in ideologies. Huxley differs from most of the other writers who express a similar concern, such as T. S. Eliot, G. Greene, E. Waugh, in that he does not see the solution to the problem in the profession of faith in one of the existing collective forms of religious belief; rather, as an apprehending individual, he seeks an approach to the divine
25 outside dogmas and recognizes it in a synthesis of what is common to all great religions.

introduced by *wenn* is not temporal, but conditional, i.e. expresses the dependence of one circumstance on another, as in this sentence, then the appropriate form in English is *if.*

1 **most significant** — wesentlichen: *substantial* in this context would mean 'large in size'; *essential* would mean 'necessary', which would be equally inappropriate. The superlative probably renders the meaning of the German best.
2 **Western** — abendländischen: *occidental* is not wrong, but it is far more common to talk of *Western literature* or *the literature of the West*.
2 **who died in** — verstorbenen: *seine verstorbene Frau* = *his late/deceased wife; seine 1972 verstorbene Frau* = *his wife, who died in 1972*. The -ed participle clause is passive, both syntactically and semantically. The verb *die* cannot, semantically, have a passive form; thus just as **she was died* is impossible, so **his wife, died in 1972* is equally impossible (see Quirk et al., p. 723).
3 **deserves** — gebührt: W. Friedrich remarks on the tendency for German sentences with an abstract subject and a reference to a person to be matched by English sentences with a personal subject (see Friederich, chapter VII: "Abstrakt-konkret", pp. 65–72).
3 **exponents** — Vertretern: *exponent* is preferable to *representative* here. In as much as he was an author of psychological novels, Huxley can be said to be an exponent of the psychological novel, but he is not a representative of the psychological novel, rather of the authors of the psychological novel.
3 **gaze** — Blick: *his gaze* implies deliberateness and intentness. *Stare, glance* and *view* are not possible. A *stare* is not produced deliberately, but occurs involuntarily, and is evoked by an emotion such as astonishment, horror or admiration. A *glance*, although possibly deliberate to a certain extent, is not sufficiently intent (*a cursory glance*). His *view* would imply either his opinion or what he could see from a certain position (*Aussicht*).
3 **penetrates** — dringt: also *pierces*, possibly *probes*, although this adds overtones of 'searching'; not *intrudes*.
4 **deep** — tief: *deep* or *deeply*? *Deep* occurs frequently in the collocation *deep down* as an intensifier pre-modifying an adverb, e.g.
Deep down inside him he despised her.
The body lay deep down at the bottom of the well.
Similarly *deep* occurs pre-modifying a prepositional phrase, e.g. *The potholers penetrated deep into the hillside*, (*deep into* being a common collocation).
Deeply occurs as an intensifier pre-modifying an adjective, e.g. *He felt deeply worried (deeply hurt)*, but *deep* is found in certain word-compounds, e.g. *Prejudice is deeply rooted. Prejudice is deep-rooted.*

In certain cases both forms are possible at the same place within a sentence, but with different functions, e.g.
He gazed deeply *into her eyes.*
He gazed deep into her eyes.
The form *deeply* describes the way in which the subject is gazing (manner adjunct) whereas *deep* intensifies the meaning of *into* (intensifier pre-modifying a prepositional phrase). In the Huxley text both forms could conceivably be possible, but the form *deep* would be the more probable.

4 **of modern man** − des modernen Menschen: a very common source of error for German students. *Man* used with generic reference, i.e. when it refers to the class 'man' and not to a specific man or men, is not preceded by an article even when the reference is to a specific genus, e.g. *Neanderthal man, primitive man.*
4 **sets down** − hält fest: also *notes, traces.*
4 **what he finds** − Befund: also *his findings;* not *diagnosis,* which is a step further in the process, namely the interpretation of the findings.
5 **pen** − Stift: also *pencil,* possibly *nib.*
5 **in spite of** − trotz: also *despite.*
5 **rationally** − vernunftmäßig: *rationally* implies using the intellect; *reasonably,* which implies sensibly, according to common sense, is not correct here.
5 **structure** − Überbaus: not *superstructure,* which is a structure built on or resting on other foundations; *overlying structure* is possible, but as *rationally conceived overlying structure* is on the long side, it would then be better to say *despite the rational conception of the overlying structure.*
5 **that characterizes** − der ... kennzeichnet: also *which characterizes* or *characteristic of.*
6 **most important** − bedeutendsten: also *most significant.*
6 **failed to create** − hat ... keine ... geschaffen: this is rather more elegant than *created no new forms* or *did not create any new forms,* although these are both grammatically correct and acceptable in this text.
He failed or *he has failed*? Leech, p. 8, remarks that there is almost free variation of Past and Present tenses when an artist who is no longer living is being discussed in connection with his work (although not in connection with biographical details of his life, e.g. *Huxley, who died in 1965*). We notice a similar use of Past and Present tenses in the German text − details verging on the biographical are expressed in the Past (*Herkunft und Persönlichkeit ließen ihn jedoch* ..., l. 16) whereas details referring to Huxley as seen through his works are presented in the Present (e.g. *er*

propagiert ..., 1. 18). It is interesting to note that the author finds it quite natural to employ both Perfect and Present tenses together in this context (*Er hat den „inneren Monolog" nicht verwendet, und er bemüht sich auch nicht* ..., 1. 10/11). The difficulty for the German student, then, lies not so much in the choice of Past and Present as in the choice of Simple Past or Present Perfect, where a past tense seems called for. Since Huxley is dead, it would be more likely that the Simple Past would be used in this case, i.e. *he failed (in his life-time) to create* ... The Perfect tense would theoretically be possible from the viewpoint that Huxley still lives through his works, but would sound rather anomalous, since explicit reference has been made to Huxley's death in the text.

6 **as ... did** — wie: English requires a clause of comparison here, therefore the verb is necessary; also possible, although with a slight change of emphasis, *Unlike James ... he failed to create new forms, in spite of* ... . Also possible *as did James, Conrad*, etc.

7 **on the contrary** — im Gegenteil: *on the contrary* and *to the contrary* are not interchangeable. *On the contrary* occurs as an antithetic conjunct (Quirk et al., p. 522) whereas *to the contrary* normally occurs as a prepositional phrase postmodifying a noun, as in the following example: *Traffic accidents haven't grown less; on the contrary, they have increased. There was a rumour that the Government intended to ban Sunday driving again, but they have just issued a statement to the contrary.* Other common collocations — *argument to the contrary, information to the contrary.*

9 **theory is often presented** — bieten sie die Theorie: see Friederich, pp. 112—116: "Das Verhältnis von Aktiv und Passiv".

9 **essay-like** — essayhaften: also *essayistic.*

9 **that could hardly be called objective** — kaum objektivierten: *objectified* exists but is only very rarely used, and although grammatically correct, would be unlikely. *Kaum objektivierten* suggests that in the author's opinion Aldous Huxley has not paid sufficient attention to presenting his theory objectively — hence the translations *in an insufficiently objective essay-like form* or *in an essay-like form that could hardly be called objective.*

10 **did not employ** — hat nicht verwendet: also *did not use.*

10 **interior monologue** — den „inneren Monolog": the usual technical term is *interior monologue*, rather than *internal/inner monologue; soliloquy* is impossible. The definite article is not normally used here, e.g. *the poet employs onomatopoeia, alliteration, hyperbole*, etc.

10 **nor did he** — und er ... auch nicht: note the inversion after *nor.*

10 **seek** — bemüht sich: also *make an attempt, make an effort, endeavour.*

11 **eradicate** – ... Austilgung: also *erase;* not *exterminate,* which is usually used in connection with animals.
11 **traces** – Spuren: not *tracks,* which refer to the marks left by people or animals, for example, in mud or in snow.
11 **of the presence of the author** – des künstlerischen Ich: possibly *the artistic self; artistic, lyrical* or *narrative I/speaker* refer to the first person in a work of art, and not to the author, with whom they are not necessarily identical.
12 **his lifelong friend** – ... lebenslängliche Freundschaft: *his lifelong friend* is neater than e.g. *with whom he was bound in lifelong friendship.*
12 **disturbed** – beunruhigt: also *worried, troubled,* not *sorry.*
13 **cerebral** – zerebralen: the use of the word is unusual in both German and English. To translate it by, say, *intellectual* would be to reduce its impact. *Brain-centred* or *brain-orientated* might be acceptable variants.
14 **resigned acceptance** – Sich-Abfinden: *coming to terms with* and *putting up with* are possible, though neither is completely satisfactory. *Adaptation to* and *apathy towards* are both a little too far away from the meaning of the German.
14 **upbringing** – Herkunft: possibly *origin; descent* would refer to ancestors and would thus go too far back in time. *Upbringing* can refer not only to the fact of being brought up but also to the manner in which it took place (SOED, p. 2319) and is thus sufficiently wide in scope to include the influence of Huxley's general social origin and of his particular family, as suggested by *Herkunft.*
15 **overcome** – überwinden: also *to find a way out of, to deal with,* but not *surmount,* which often collocates with *obstacles* or *difficulties.*
16 **human nature in its entirety** – totale menschliche Natur: possibly *the whole of human nature* or *human nature in its totality.*
17 **saving** – Rettung: also *the salvation of,* which has rather stronger religious connotations. *Salvage* is used principally of the saving of a ship or its cargo from damage or loss at sea.
18 **spiritual man** – geistigen Menschen: *geistig* can often be translated by *intellectual.* However, it is evident from the text that Huxley is not concerned with man as a rational being (as opposed to a non-rational being) but man as having an existence on an immaterial level (as opposed to having existence solely on a material level); *intellectual* would therefore be inappropriate. Another possible translation would be *man's soul.*
19 **present-day** – heutigen: also *in/under the conditions of today.*
19 **wither away** – verkümmern: also *fade away* or *decline,* although these are not as strong; *dwindle* is too weak.

20 **deceptive** — trügerische: also *delusory, delusive;* not *deceitful,* which implies a will or intention to deceive.
21 **writers** — Dichtern: also *authors; poet* usually refers only to a writer of poetry, and therefore cannot be used here as Greene and Waugh are not primarily writers of poetry.
21 **such as** — wie: *such as* expresses apposition and is related in meaning to *for example, for instance; as* is impossible here.
22 **to the problem** — des Problems: not *of the problem.*
23 **profession of faith in** — Bekenntnis zu: also *acceptance of, acknowledgement of.* These lack the religious connotations of *Bekenntnis* and its rendering as *profession of faith,* yet in a way they are more suitable because they express the fact of accepting a belief as a solution to the problem, whereas *profession of faith* stresses the action of declaring one's faith after its acceptance.

---

2. Treibhaus der Traditionen

Verpaßt Großbritannien den Anschluß an die moderne Welt? Deutsche, die England bewundern, vergleichen nicht selten mit wehmütigem Neid die Atmosphäre eines Landes, in dem sich historische Kontinuität so vielfältig äußert, mit der traditionslosen Realität der Bundesrepublik.

Aber ist der Fluch britischer Tradition nicht tatsächlich viel augenfälliger als ihr Segen? Es geht nicht bloß darum, daß so viele Traditionen im Grunde längst anachronistisch geworden sind. Gefährlicher ist die Pflege eines Geistes, der dem Alten den Vorzug vor dem Neuen gibt, und allzu oft sich dem Schein zuwendet, nicht dem Sein. Schein, historisches Theater beherrschen geradezu das politische Leben. Das schlagendste Beispiel ist „die gnädige Rede vom Thron", mit der alljährlich im Herbst die neue Parlamentssaison eröffnet wird. Die Königin verliest die Rede vom Thron im Oberhaus. Das Unterhaus muß warten, bis der Herold, der „schwarze Stab", erscheint, um die „Commoners" aufzufordern, an der Schranke des Oberhauses zu erscheinen.

Dann traben sie hinüber, geführt vom Premierminister und dem Führer der „treuen Opposition ihrer Majestät", und stehen — sie, welche die wahre und einzige Macht in dieser repräsentativen Demokratie verkörpern — hinten zusammengedrängt, während die edlen Lords, die so gut wie keine Macht mehr haben, auf den Bänken sitzen. Und die Königin verkündet Regierungspläne in Worten, die alle vom Premierminister stammen, und die sie aussprechen muß, ob sie will oder nicht; denn wenn sie nicht wollte, müßte

24 **apprehending** — erlebendes: also *aware, conscious.*
24 **he seeks an approach** — er sucht den Zugang: also *he seeks access to, he strives for admittance to;* not *entrance.*
25 **outside** — außerhalb: possibly *beyond,* not *extra.*
25 **of what** — dessen, was: also *that which,* but not **that what.*

Relative clauses
One of the most frequently occurring mistakes in this text was the wrong use of commas with relative clauses.

A non-defining clause is separated off from its antecedent by a comma, but there is no comma between a necessary, or defining, relative clause and its antecedent.

The wrong use of commas obscures the relations between the parts of the sentence and thus misleads the reader, or even alters the meaning of the sentence completely.

---

2. Hothouse of Tradition

Is Great Britain failing to link up with the modern world? It is not uncommon for Germans who admire England to compare with melancholy envy the atmosphere of a country where historical continuity is expressed in so many ways with the reality of the Federal Republic, which is so lacking in
5 tradition.

Yet are the disadvantages of British traditions not in fact far more evident than their advantages? The point is not just that so many traditions have, strictly speaking, long since become anachronistic. What is more dangerous is the cultivation of a spirit which prefers the old to the new and all too often
10 turns to show instead of facing reality. Show and pageantry virtually dominate political life. The most striking example is "the gracious speech from the throne" which marks the annual autumn opening of the new parliamentary session. The Queen reads out the speech from the throne in the House of Lords. The House of Commons must wait until the herald,
15 "Black Rod", appears to summon the Commoners to the bar of the House of Lords.

Then they trot across, led by the Prime Minister and the Leader of Her Majesty's Loyal Opposition, to stand crammed together at the back — they who embody the true and only power in this representative democracy —
20 while the noble lords, who have virtually no power left, sit in the benches. And the Queen announces Government plans in the Prime Minister's words,

nicht der hinten stehende Premierminister abdanken, sondern sie, die auf dem Thron sitzt. Wenn die Tradition solchen historischen Theaters zur allgemeinen Vorstellung beiträgt, daß sich im Grunde seit den glorreichen alten Zeiten nicht gar so viel geändert habe, so schadet sie einem Volk, das vor allem begreifen muß, wie viel sich geändert hat.

Aus: E. Wolf, *Treibhaus der Traditionen*, in: *Die Zeit* 31/1965.

Commentary

Hothouse of Tradition — Treibhaus der Traditionen: here we have the title of a newspaper article, aimed at catching the reader's eye by the use of an unusual metaphor, reinforced by alliteration. The problem for the translator is whether to sacrifice the alliteration and translate the metaphor, if there is a suitable English equivalent, or to substitute a different metaphor which retains the alliteration.

If we choose to retain the metaphor (*Treibhaus*), we have the choice between *glass-house, greenhouse, forcing-house, hot-bed, conservatory*, or *hothouse*, all of which have been offered in students' translations. We have to choose the word which best suggests the qualities of protection, preservation and encouragement of growth suggested by *Treibhaus*. *Glass-house* can be used metaphorically, but its connotations make it unsuitable here. "People who live in glass-houses ..." (proverb) = 'people whose own reputations are fragile'; *to live in a glass-house* = 'to be permanently on show, in the public eye'. The prosaic *greenhouse* would seem incongruous used metaphorically. A *forcing-house* is used not just to encourage growth, but to force unnaturally fast growth and is thus inappropriate. *Hot-bed* is often used metaphorically, but usually with negative associations, e.g. *a hot-bed of revolution, a hot-bed of corruption.* A *conservatory*, often built directly onto a house and containing seats, has similarities to the German *Wintergarten. Hothouse*, which has all the connotations of protection, preservation and encouragement of growth, seems to be the best choice.

If we choose to retain the alliteration of the German through substituting another metaphor, we might choose something like *trustee of tradition* or *treasure-house of tradition*. By substituting *custom* for *tradition*, and using *conservatory*, which in its more general use can mean 'a place for conserving', we might render *Treibhaus der Traditionen* by *Conservatory*

which she is obliged to utter, whether she wants to or not; for if she were to refuse, it would be she sitting on the throne, and not the Prime Minister standing at the back, who would have to resign office.

25 If the tradition of such pageantry contributes to the general notion that basically not really very much has changed since the glorious times of old, then this tradition harms a nation that above all must comprehend how much actually has changed.

of Custom and thus retain both alliteration and metaphor, though at the cost of weakening the metaphor. *Tradition* or *traditions*? Both are possible, but the generic uncountable form would be more probable here than the countable *traditions* (Quirk et al., p. 153).

1 **Is Great Britain failing to link up with ...** — Verpaßt Großbritannien den Anschluß ...: also *failing to connect up with. Verpaßt Großbritannien den Anschluß* can suggest an action covering a temporary period of time starting in the past and extending into the future — temporary because in the author's opinion there will come a point by which Great Britain either will have connected up with the modern world, or will definitely have failed to do so. The limited duration of this period would normally be expressed in English by the use of the progressive aspect. The difficulty here lies in the fact that the translation the majority of students offered — *miss the connection* — involves a verb which expresses a momentary event that cannot have duration. The event is so brief that it is no sooner present than it is past — *he's going to miss his connection, he has missed his connection*. The Present Progressive (used to express duration) and *miss the connection* (momentary event) are thus incompatible. We can avoid this problem by using *fail to link up with/fail to connect up with* as *fail* can be used in the Present Progressive form in the sense of *being on the path to failure*. The Simple Present form (*does Great Britain fail ...*) would imply *does Great Britain regularly*, i.e. every week, every year, etc., *fail ...* and is thus inappropriate.

Verpaßt can also be interpreted as having a future reference. In this case, the version *will Great Britain fail to link up ...* is preferable for stylistic reasons to *is Great Britain going to fail to link up/is Great Britain about to fail to link up* because these latter both contain a repetition of *to* + infinitive.

The versions *failing to keep in touch with, becoming out of touch with, losing contact/touch with* all suggest that Great Britain already had contact with the modern world, which is not implied by the text. *Failing to keep up with,* or *failing to keep pace with* might be possible, although neither include the aspect of 'linking' contained in the German.

1 **it is not uncommon** — nicht selten: also *it is not rare,* or *Germans who admire England not infrequently/not uncommonly compare* ... The use of the double negative is a device for understatement. *Not seldom* and *not rarely*, however, would be unusual collocations and are best avoided. *Not* modifies the adverb, not the verb, therefore the inclusion of the auxiliary *do* as in **do not infrequently compare* is wrong. The version *Germans who admire England are not infrequently filled with melancholy envy when they compare* ... has the advantage of integrating *melancholy envy* neatly into the sentence, but the slight disadvantage that it links *not infrequently* with *filled with melancholy envy* rather than with *compare*, as in the German text.

2 **Germans who admire England** — Deutsche, die England bewundern: note that this is a defining relative clause, specifying a particular group of people, and as such is not separated from the rest of the sentence by commas. The insertion of commas (*Germans, who admire England,*) would alter the meaning radically: *Germans — and by the way all Germans admire England —.*

It is often possible to use a post-modifying *-ing* participle construction in the place of a defining relative clause. The *-ing* participle in this type of non-finite post-modifying clause need not correspond to a progressive form in the finite defining relative clause. In other words, stative verbs which normally do not occur in the progressive aspect can occur as post-modifying *-ing* participles. Quirk gives as an example (p.876) *He is talking to a girl resembling Joan* (*who resembles Joan*, not **who is resembling Joan*).

Nevertheless, we have deliberately avoided the form *Germans admiring England* for the following reasons. *Admire* can be used both to express a state (*I admire Constable's paintings*) and to express an event (*What are you doing? I'm admiring your paintings* in the sense of 'looking at/contemplating with admiration', and *the group stopped in front of a painting and admired it loudly* i.e. 'expressed their admiration').

The use of the *-ing* participle in *Germans admiring England* is awkward as although theoretically *admiring* can convey both the state and the event meanings of *admire,* in fact the event meanings, being more closely associated with the *-ing* form, tend to dominate, and *Germans admiring England* seems to suggest *Germans (who are) expressing their admiration for England* (see also Leech, states and events, p.4 ff; multiple class membership, p.22 ff). It is of course possible to avoid the difficulty completely by using *German admirers of* ...

2 **England**: note that the author, in common with many others, equates Great Britain with England. Great Britain is composed of Scotland, England, N. Ireland and Wales, and it is incorrect to talk of England if Britain is meant.

2 **melancholy** — wehmütigem: also *sad;* not *wistful,* which adds an element of longing to the German; not *nostalgic,* which implies looking back with longing to something one already had, or had experienced.

3 **of a country where** — eines Landes, in dem: also *in which.* NB This is a defining relative clause, and as such is not separated off by commas.

3 **historical** — historische: *historical* means 'related to, concerning, or dealing with history', as in *historical novel.* The use of *historic* is much narrower; SOED gives "noted or celebrated in history" as "the prevailing current usage" (p.906). Commonly found in collocations such as *a historic event/occasion/moment.* Whereas *historical events* are events in history, *historic events* are events of importance in history.

3 **is expressed** — sich ... äußert: also *expresses itself, is manifested.*

4 **so lacking in tradition** — traditionslosen: also *so bare of, so devoid of;* *traditionless does not exist.

6 **yet** — aber: also *but.*

6 **disadvantages, advantages** — Fluch, Segen: also *curse, blessing.*

6 **evident** — augenfällig: also *obvious, noticeable.*

7 **The point is not just ...** — Es geht nicht bloß darum ...: also *the problem/the question is not just ...*

8 **strictly speaking** — im Grunde: also *in effect.*

8 **have ... long since become** — längst ... geworden sind: if *long since* is used, then the verb will be in the Perfect form, as *since* indicates a period of past time leading up to the present. *Long ago* or *a long time ago* refer to a period of time completed in the past and are accompanied by the Simple Past form of the verb.

8 **What is more dangerous is ...** — Gefährlicher ist ...: also *a greater danger is presented by ..., more dangerous is ..., the cultivation of ... presents a great danger.*

9 **cultivation** — Pflege: not *culture.*

9 **prefers** — den Vorzug gibt: also *which puts the old before the new* or *which*

gives the old priority over the new. Common mistakes: *which puts the old in front of the new,* **which prefers the old before the new.*

9 **the old to the new** — dem Alten ... dem Neuen: also *what is old to what is new.*

10 **show, reality** — Schein, Sein: English does not seem to possess a corresponding 'minimal pair', so alternatives must be sought. *Appearances* or *outer appearances* could replace *show* in this sentence, but *Schein* also appears in the following sentence (*Schein, historisches Theater*) and *show* collocates better with *pageantry* than *appearances* does. If *appearances* is used, then *retreats behind appearances* is possible.

10 **pageantry** — historisches Theater: *historical theatre* is impossible, as *theatre* cannot be used in this sense of the German *Theater*. *Historical play-acting* would be possible, but would add derogatory overtones of meaning.

10 **virtually** — geradezu: also *practically; almost* is not quite strong enough.

11 **dominate** — beherrschen: also *rule, govern.*

11 **political life** — das politische Leben: zero article in English, as *political life* is unrestricted. Prepositional post-modification by an *of*-phrase, which restricts the noun phrase, would require the definite article, e.g. *the political life of England, the political life of Disraeli.*

Other post-modifying prepositional phrases are not regarded as being equally restrictive, and do not necessarily require the definite article, e.g. *political life in England, political life after the Restoration, political life under the Stuarts* (see also Quirk et al., p.153).

12 **which marks the opening** — mit der ... eröffnet wird: also *which opens ...* or *by/with which ... is opened.*

12 **the annual autumn** — alljährlich im Herbst: as this really modifies the fact of the opening of the new session rather than the marking of the opening by the Queen's Speech, it can be translated adjectivally as *which marks the annual autumn opening of ...* or as a post-modifying prepositional or adverbial phrase — *the opening of ... in the autumn of every year/every autumn/every year in autumn. Annually* and *yearly* would be felt to modify the verb *mark* and thus seem awkward.

13 **parliamentary session** — Parlamentssaison: not *season, term. Term* can be used in a parliamentary context, for example, *the Prime Minister's term of office is drawing to a close,* but is not appropriate here.

13 **reads out** — verliest: not *makes a speech.* This would imply that the Queen reads out her own speech, whereas in fact she reads out a speech prepared by the Prime Minister; *proclaim* and *pronounce* are both unsuitable.

14 **House of Lords, House of Commons** — Oberhaus, Unterhaus: *upper house/chamber, lower house/chamber* exist with reference to other

governments, but in a specifically British context it would be normal to use *House of Lords* and *House of Commons*.
15 **Black Rod** – der „schwarze Stab": "Short for *Gentleman Usher of the Black Rod*, so called from his symbol of office. The chief Gentleman usher of the Lord Chamberlain's department of the royal household, and also usher to the House of Lords, and to the Chapter of the Garter" (SOED p. 185). The noun *usher* in its modern use is mainly confined to denoting a man who shows people to their seats, e.g. at a concert, large meeting, in a church. *Usherette* denotes a woman who shows people to their seats, usually in a cinema or a theatre.
15 **appears to summon** – erscheint, ... aufzufordern, ... zu erscheinen: the repetition of *appear* is not necessary in English as *summon (aufzufordern)* implies 'summon to appear'.
15 **to summon** – aufzufordern: *summon* best suits the traditional nature of the context. *Order* and *command* both imply too large a degree of compulsion – after all, the Commoners presumably wish to enter the House of Lords, and are waiting to be called.
15 **bar** – Schranke: this particular *Schranke* is commonly known as the *bar*, therefore other versions, such as *barrier*, are impossible.
17 **trot across** – traben hinüber: also *trot over;* not to be confused with *tread, trod, trodden*.
17 **led by** – geführt vom: also *headed by*.
18 **Loyal** – treuen: 'Loyal Opposition' is the common collocation; *true* and *faithful* are therefore not appropriate here.
18 **to stand** – und stehen: also *and stand*.
18 **crammed together** – zusammengedrängt: also *crushed, crowded, packed, squeezed, squashed, herded;* not *cramped*, which can apply to an individual being severely limited in his movements, but not to a group of individuals in their spatial relationship to one another.
18 **at the back** – hinten: also *at/in the rear*.
19 **who embody** – sie, welche ... verkörpern: although this clause could occur between *stand* and *crammed together* in the English version as in the German version, it is probably stylistically preferable to place it after *crammed together at the back*, rather than interrupt the short clause by the insertion of a longer clause.
19 **embody** – verkörpern: also *constitute, represent;* not *incorporate*.
20 **virtually no power left** – so gut wie keine Macht mehr: variants: *almost/practically no power left, hardly/scarcely any power left*. Not **nearly no power left*. Although *almost* can co-occur with *no* and *none*

(e.g. there are almost none left), *nearly* normally doesn't (e.g. * there are nearly none left).
20 **in the benches** — auf den Bänken: *in* or *on the benches*? The choice of preposition is a matter of view-point. If the bench is seen mainly in terms of its flat horizontal surface, then it is something to sit *on* (similarly *he was sitting on a hard chair, on a stool, on a park-bench*). If the bench is seen as an enclosed area containing seating facilities, then it is something to sit *in* (similarly *he was sitting in the third pew, in the back row*). If the seat has 'embracing' qualities, then it is also something to sit *in* (*he was sitting in an armchair, in a deck-chair, in a wheel-chair*). Not *banks*.
21 **Government plans** — Regierungspläne: also *the plans of the Government, the Government's plans*.
21 **in the Prime Minister's words** — in Worten, die alle vom Premierminister stammen: also *in words which all come from/originate from the Prime Minister, from a text drafted by the Prime Minister*.
22 **is obliged to** — muß: *must* is also possible, but *obliged to* is semantically more stressed than *must*, which if this text were spoken, would receive an intonational stress.
22 **whether she wants to or not** — ob sie will oder nicht: also ... *is willing or not, ... likes it or not*.
22 **if she were to refuse** — wenn sie nicht wollte: *if she refused* is possible, but *were to* in *if she were to refuse* increases the improbability of her refusing.

---

3. Der Film im Fremdsprachenunterricht

Der audiolingual fundierte Fremdsprachenunterricht geht u. a. davon aus, daß die systematische Entwicklung des Hörverstehens einen wichtigen Beitrag zur Entwicklung sprachlicher Fertigkeiten darstellt. Hier wird der Film — schließt man die Übersetzung bewußt aus — zum notwendigen Teilbestand eines fremdsprachlichen Lehrgangs, der die Umgangssprache, d. h. Dialoge in konkreten Situationen, zum Lernziel erhebt und darum auch von Dialogen in konkreten Situationen ausgehen muß. Corder hat überzeugend dargelegt, daß Sprache nicht eindeutig und umfassend verstanden werden kann, wenn die nichtlinguistischen Faktoren einer Situation nur unvollkommen dargeboten werden oder ganz fehlen. Eindeutigkeit des Verständnisses aber muß gewährleistet sein, wenn es um Einführung und Erstdarbietung geht. Hier stellt der Film — abgesehen einmal von den thematisch stark begrenzten und nur laienhaft simulierten, oft peinlichen Spielszenen in der Klasse — die

Also possible: *if she didn't wish to do so, if she were unwilling to do so, if she wouldn't do so* (*wouldn't* in this case is a Past form of *will*, not the Conditional, and carries the meaning 'refused').

23 **sitting on the throne** — die auf dem Thron sitzt: also *seated on the throne*.
24 **resign office** — abdanken: *abdanken* refers to both the Queen and the Prime Minister. *Abdicate* would be inappropriate as a translation as it means *give up the throne* and therefore can only apply to the Queen. Similarly *resign (from) one's post* can only strictly speaking apply to the Prime Minister, as the Queen does not hold a 'post'. *Office*, however, can apply to both.
25 **notion** — Vorstellung: also *idea, belief*.
26 **the glorious times of old** — den glorreichen alten Zeiten: also *glorious old days, glorious days of old/of yore*, possibly *good old days*, although this suggests times that were enjoyable rather than glorious.
27 **harms** — schadet: also *damages;* variant: *then it is a tradition that harms a nation...*; also Present Progressive, which would stress the immediacy rather than the permanency of the harming.
27 **a nation** — einem Volk: also *a people*. Both *who* and *which* would be acceptable as relative pronouns here, depending on whether *nation* and *people* are seen as collections of individuals (*who*) or as units (*which*).
28 **actually**: optional; this has been added to give more stress to the final clause. *Actually* could also be placed between the auxiliary and the Past Participle.

---

3. The Film in Foreign Language Teaching

Foreign language teaching based on the audiolingual method takes as one of its premises that the systematic training of listening comprehension forms an important contribution to the development of language skills. If translation is deliberately excluded, then the film becomes a necessary component of a
5 foreign language course which elevates colloquial language, i.e. dialogues in concrete situations, to the status of a teaching objective, and therefore has to take dialogues in concrete situations as its starting-point. Corder has convincingly demonstrated that language cannot be unambiguously and comprehensively understood if the non-linguistic factors of a situation are
10 only imperfectly presented or indeed are totally absent. Comprehension must be guaranteed and misinterpretation ruled out during the introduction and initial presentation phases. Leaving aside scenes acted out in class, which are extremely limited in theme, amateurishly performed and often embarrassing,

einzige adäquate Form dar, um über Sehen und Hören zum Verstehen zu führen. Gleichzeitig leistet er einen weiteren, für die Lernziele eines audiolingualen Sprachunterrichts unverzichtbaren Beitrag: indem er nichtverbale Situationen der umgangssprachlichen Wirklichkeit bereitstellt, auf die Schüler sprachlich reagieren können.

Aus: R. Freudenstein, *Die Funktion des Films im fremdsprachlichen Unterricht*, in: H. S. Ankerstein (Hg.), *Das visuelle Element im Fremdsprachenunterricht*. Stuttgart: Ernst Klett, 1972.

Commentary

1 **based on the audiolingual method** — audiolingual fundierte: also *based on audiolingual principles/on audiolingual teaching theory*. Possibly *founded*, but not *grounded.*
Grounded occurs most frequently in collocations such as
a) a well-grounded argument (= based on sound reasons)
b) to be well-grounded in a subject (= to have a good knowledge of basic facts)
c) a ship grounded in the storm (= ran aground)
d) the pilot was grounded (= forbidden to fly).

1 **takes as one of its premises** — geht u. a. davon aus: here there are several possible versions, for example, *starts among other things from the assumption that, is based ... on the assumption that, takes as one of its basic assumptions the theory that,* or *one of the basic assumptions of audiolingual language teaching is that*. u(nter) a(nderem): either included in the noun phrase *as one of its ...* or *among other things*. Not *among others*, which implies *among other people*, e.g. *several people – John among others – witnessed the accident.*

2 **systematic** — systematische: not *systematical*, which SOED refers to as "now rare or obsolete" (p. 2116).

2 **listening comprehension** — Hörverstehens: *listening comprehension* and *aural comprehension* are the most frequently used 'technical terms'. It would also be possible to say *auditory comprehension* or *auditive language perception.*

3 **language skills** — sprachlicher Fertigkeiten: also often referred to as *linguistic skills*, although this use is regarded as incorrect by purists, who reserve *linguistic* for uses pertaining solely to the science of language. *Skill* is the 'technical term'; *abilities, capabilities* are not appropriate.

the only form adequate to lead via seeing and hearing to understanding is the
15 film. At the same time it provides a further contribution indispensable to the
teaching objectives of audiolingual language teaching by presenting non-verbal
situations in which the language of everyday reality is used and to which
pupils can react verbally.

3 **if ... is excluded** – schließt man ... aus: the *if* clause is better placed before rather than in the middle of the main clause.
3 **translation** – die Übersetzung: *translation* as a countable noun signifies a translated text, e.g. *there must be thousands of translations of Shakespeare's works.* As an uncountable noun it signifies the process of translation, and as such, is only preceded by the definite article when a specific process of translation is being referred to, e.g. *the translation of Shakespeare's works has interested scholars for centuries.* Translation here bears its uncountable meaning, and being unspecified, is not preceded by the definite article.
4 **deliberately** – bewußt: *bewußt* in this context implies 'with intention', and thus *consciously,* implying 'in full awareness', is inappropriate here.
4 **necessary component** – notwendigen Teilbestand: also *essential part/element,* possibly *integral part.*
5 **elevates ... to the status of** – erhebt: also *raises. To the status of* is an optional addition.
5 **colloquial language** – Umgangssprache: this implies common, everyday language as opposed to a more formal language, whereas *vernacular* implies the native language of a country or region as opposed to a foreign language, and is therefore inappropriate; *everyday language* would be possible.
6 **in concrete situations** – in konkreten Situationen: also possible *contextualized (dialogues).*
6 **teaching objective** – Lernziel: this is an example of different viewpoints in the two languages. German sees the aim or objective from the pupil's point of view as 'learning objectives', whereas English usually regards it from the teacher's point of view as a teaching aim or objective.

7 **has demonstrated** — hat dargelegt: also *has shown*.
9 **factors** — Faktoren: also *features*.
10 **only imperfectly** — nur unvollkommen: also *only partially, inadequately, incompletely*.
10 **are totally absent** — ganz fehlen: also *completely missing, totally lacking*. A common mistake is the use of *at all* here as a translation for *ganz*. *At all* only occurs in conjunction with a negative, which is not the case here.
10 **comprehension must be guaranteed and misinterpretation ruled out** — Eindeutigkeit des Verständnisses aber muß gewährleistet sein: the incompatibility between the two terms *Eindeutigkeit* and *Verständnis* seems greater in English than in German — the object of comprehension (a picture, text, film, etc.) may be unambiguous or ambiguous, i.e. may offer only one or more than one interpretation, but comprehension itself cannot be ambiguous/unambiguous. There are two possibilities open to the translator depending on his purpose in translating: either he reproduces the incompatibility in English (e.g. *unequivocal/unambiguous understanding*) or he 'improves' on the text by paraphrasing (see also *unambiguously/eindeutig* in the previous sentence).
11 **guaranteed** — gewährleistet: also *assured*.
11 **during ... phases** — wenn es um ... geht: also *as far as ... are concerned*.
12 **initial presentation** — Erstdarbietung: also *first presentation,* or *introductory presentation* if *introduction* has not already been used for *Einführung*.
12 **leaving aside** — abgesehen von: also *apart from*. This clause is better placed at the beginning of the sentence than inserted in the main clause. The pre-modifying sequence in German is too long for English, and must be rendered by other means, e.g. by a relative clause.

---

4. Über den Lernprozeß

Vom sozial-kulturellen Standpunkt aus zeigt sich der Lernprozeß vorwiegend als eine Wechselwirkung zwischen dem Lernenden und seinen Mitmenschen, durch die er gleichzeitig die kulturell-geistige Tradition seiner Umwelt kennenlernt. Vom ersten Augenblick seines Lebens an ist der Mensch auf hilfsbereite erwachsene Mitmenschen angewiesen, die ihm nicht nur seine körperlichen Bedürfnisse befriedigen, sondern ihm auch helfen, nach und nach die Fertigkeiten und Mittel zum seelisch-geistigen Verständnis seiner Welt zu erwerben. Hierher gehören insbesondere die Sprache, das Denken in

12 **in class** — in der Klasse: English distinguishes between *classroom* and *class*, the latter being the group of pupils who have their lessons together. Here it is possible to say either *in class*, which means in the presence of the other pupils during lessons (similarly *in church, in school*, etc., see Quirk et al., p. 157) or *in the classroom*, but it is not possible in this context to say *in the class*.

13 **extremely limited** — stark begrenzten: also *severely limited/restricted*; not *strongly*, which as an intensifier tends to co-occur with verbs in the semantic class of 'repudiation' or 'refutation', e.g. *I strongly deny, disagree, object*, etc.

13 **amateurishly performed** — laienhaft simulierten: also *amateurishly presented, amateur in their presentation*. Not *simulated*.

14 **adequate to lead** — adäquate Form ... zu führen: also *that can adequately lead ...*

14 **via** — über: also *by way of*, not *over*.

14 **seeing and hearing** — Sehen und Hören: also *looking and listening*, which, since they imply an active involvement on the part of the pupil rather than passive perception, as in *seeing and hearing*, imply a certain degree of intention.

15 **at the same time** — gleichzeitig: not *simultaneously*, which refers to the same moment in actual time, e.g. *we started to speak simultaneously*.

17 **the language of everyday reality** — der umgangssprachlichen Wirklichkeit: not *colloquial reality*.

18 **verbally** — sprachlich: also possibly *linguistically* (compare our comments on the use of *linguistic* above).

---

4. On the Process of Learning

From the socio-cultural point of view the learning process reveals itself to be predominantly an interaction between the learner and his fellow men, through whom he at the same time becomes acquainted with the cultural and intellectual tradition of his environment. From the first moment of his life
5 the individual is dependent on the aid of adult fellow human beings who not only satisfy his physical needs but also help him gradually to acquire the skills and means to comprehend his world emotionally and intellectually. To these skills and means belong in particular speech, the ability to think in the

den Kategorien der jeweiligen Mitwelt und die ganze Reihe der Fertigkeiten, die nötig sind, um ein Leben in der menschlichen Gemeinschaft zu führen.

Auf dieser Ebene wird also Lernen zu einem äußerst komplexen Vorgang, der nicht nur durch intellektuelle Faktoren bestimmt wird, sondern vor allem auch durch emotionale, vitale und soziale Komponenten. Dies wird noch deutlicher, wenn man bedenkt, daß sich Lernen nicht mehr in der Form der individuellen Unterweisung vollzieht, sondern typischerweise in einer Gruppe.

Aus: W. Correll, *Lernpsychologie. Grundfragen und pädagogische Konsequenzen.* Donauwörth: Auer, 1969 (1961).

Commentary

On— über: although it is possible to say *a book about* or *on the process of learning,* the preposition *on* is conventionally used in titles.

1 **socio-cultural** — sozial-kulturellen: the translation of such compound adjectives into English is often problematical. (In this text we also have *kulturell-geistig* (1. 3) and *seelisch-geistig* (1. 7)). The problem lies firstly in establishing the relationship between the two parts of the compound in the German, and secondly in finding a suitable way of expressing the relationship in English. The main types of relationship are additive and modifying. In the above example the meaning is, presumably, additive. Thus we can say *social and cultural* or, as the combining form *socio-* exists, *socio-cultural (socio-* can have both additive and modifying meanings). *Social-cultural,* however, would be very unusual.

An example of *sozial-* in a modifying relationship would be *sozial-politisch* (also *sozialpolitisch*). A translation of *sozial-politische Überlegungen* might possibly be *socio-political considerations,* but would probably be *considerations of social policy.* It would not, however, be *social and political considerations,* which has a different (additive) meaning.

1 **reveals itself to be** — zeigt sich als: also *appears to be, is seen to be.* Not *shows itself.*

2 **predominantly** — vorwiegend: also *mainly, principally.*

2 **interaction** — Wechselwirkung: also possibly *action and reaction, reciprocal action.* Not *action and counteraction* or *counter-reaction,* as *counter-* implies some sort of opposition and resistance. *Counter-reaction* also seems tautological.

2 **fellow men** — Mitmenschen: not *contemporaries,* which lays too much emphasis on the aspect of 'living at the same time' rather than 'living

categories of the society in question, and the whole range of skills necessary
10 for leading a life in the human community.
   Learning at this level thus becomes an extremely complex process which is determined not only by intellectual factors but also, above all, by emotional, vital and social components. This becomes clearer still when one considers that learning no longer takes place in the form of individual instruction but
15 typically in a group.

together', and also might suggest 'of roughly the same age', which is certainly not suggested by the text.
3 **through whom** — durch die: 50% of the students interpreted *durch die* as referring to *Mitmenschen,* whereas the other 50% interpreted it as referring to *Wechselwirkung*. In the first case, the translation would be *through whom* but not *by whom*; in the second case either *by which* or *through which*.
3 **cultural and intellectual** — kulturell-geistige: another compound adjective (see above). Here again the compound is presumably additive. *Cultural* normally has no combining form parallel to *socio-*. Not *cultural-intellectual*. Note that the translation of *geistige* here by *spiritual* is not appropriate. *Spiritual* normally occurs in religious, philosophical or supernatural contexts.
4 **from the first moment of his life** — vom ersten Augenblick seines Lebens an: not *from the early beginning* ... or *from the (very) first beginning* ..., which are tautological. *From the very beginning* ... would be possible.
5 **dependent on the aid of ... fellow human beings** — auf hilfsbereite ... Mitmenschen angewiesen: *helpful ... human beings* would be possible, but *helpful* tends to be used in more trivial situations than this. *Willing to help* would also be possible, but would need to be used in a relative clause, thus giving us *dependent on human beings who are willing to help and who* ..., which is rather clumsy. *Dependent on the willingness/readiness to help of* ... is also possible, though this lays perhaps a shade too much emphasis on the readiness rather than on the help. Our version *dependent on the aid of* ... errs perhaps too much in the other direction, but has the advantage of grammatical simplicity.

5 **adult** – erwachsene: *grown-up* is rather colloquial, and usually said by children or by adults when speaking to or writing for children. Better avoided in this type of context.
5 **not only ... but also** – nicht nur..., sondern auch: care must be taken with the position of these coordinating correlatives. They immediately precede what they coordinate. Here they coordinate two clauses *satisfy ...* and *help ...*, and thus precede them. *Human beings who satisfy not only his physical needs* is wrong here. This would be expected to go on something like ... *and also his emotional needs*.
6 **physical** – körperlichen: also *bodily*.
6 **gradually** – nach und nach: also *step by step*. Not *by and by*, which implies after a short period of time. (*I'll do it by and by* = 'I'll do it in a few minutes/when I have the time').
7 **means to comprehend his world** – Mittel zum Verständnis seiner Welt: also *means for a ... understanding/comprehension of his world*.
7 **emotionally and intellectually** – seelisch-geistigen: students were divided on their interpretation of this. To some *seelisch* modified *geistig*, thus narrowing or making more specific its meaning. For the majority, however, the relationship between the two parts was additive and expressed a certain opposition between two faculties of the mind, the affective (*seelisch*) and the cognitive (*geistig*), hence the translation *emotional(ly) and intellectual(ly)*. *Rational* would also be possible as a variant for

---

5. Die deutsche Bildungskatastrophe

Eines der tragenden Fundamente jedes modernen Staates ist sein Bildungswesen. Niemand müßte das besser wissen als die Deutschen. Der Aufstieg Deutschlands in den Kreis der großen Kulturnationen wurde im neunzehnten Jahrhundert durch den Ausbau der Universitäten und der Schulen begründet. Bis zum Ersten Weltkrieg beruhten die politische Stellung Deutschlands, seine wirtschaftliche Blüte und die Entfaltung seiner Industrie auf seinem damals modernen Schulsystem und auf den Leistungen einer Wissenschaft, die Weltgeltung erlangt hatte. Wir zehren bis heute von diesem Kapital. Die wirtschaftliche und politische Führungsschicht, die das sogenannte Wirtschaftswunder ermöglicht hat, ist vor dem Ersten Weltkrieg in die Schule gegangen; die Kräfte, die heute Wirtschaft und Gesellschaft tragen, verdanken ihre geistige Formung den Schulen und Universitäten der Weimarer Zeit. Jetzt aber ist das Kapital verbraucht: Die Bundesrepublik steht in der vergleichen-

intellectual. Spiritual (to translate *seelisch*) is inappropriate here (see above). *Psychic* or *psychical* (to translate *seelisch*) in their general meaning referring to the mind or soul tend to occur mainly in highly specialized philosophical or psychological contexts. Moreover they refer to the mind or soul rather than to an aspect of the mind or soul, and thus cannot be used in opposition to *intellectual*. *Psychic* and *psychical* are most widely known in their special sense, namely when restricted to unusual mental phenomena such as telepathy, second sight, mediums.

9 **in question** — jeweiligen: *respective* cannot be used here as it only occurs in a plural noun phrase, and with reference to another plural or coordinate noun phrase, e.g. *the children ran to their respective mothers* (see Quirk et al., p. 614—15). Variant: *of the particular society*.

9 **range** — Reihe: not *line;* not *lot,* which is too colloquial.

12 **not only ... but also** — nicht nur ..., sondern auch: see above. Here these correlatives coordinate *intellektuelle Faktoren* and *emotionale Komponenten,* and thus must directly precede them. The position of *not only* in *... which are not only determined by intellectual factors ...* is therefore wrong.

14 **no longer** — nicht mehr: a verb preceded by *no longer* does not require the auxiliary *do/does*. It would be possible to use the form *not ... any longer (does not take place any longer),* but this would be more appropriate to the spoken language.

---

5. Germany's Educational Catastrophe

One of the essential foundations of every modern state is its educational system. Nobody should know this better than the Germans. Germany's rise into the circle of the great cultural nations was founded on the expansion of the universities and schools in the 19th century. Up to the First World War
5 Germany's political position, its economic prosperity and the growth of its industry were based on its then modern school-system and on the achievements of a science which had gained world-wide renown. We are still drawing on that capital. The economic and political leaders who made possible the so-called economic miracle went to school before the
10 First World War; the men on whom economy and society today depend were intellectually shaped by the schools and universities of the Weimar Period. Now, however, the capital has been exhausted: in comparative statistics on education, the Federal Republic ranges at the lower end of the European

den Schulstatistik am unteren Ende der europäischen Länder neben Jugoslawien, Irland, Portugal. Die jungen Wissenschaftler wandern zu Tausenden aus, weil sie in ihrem Vaterland nicht mehr die Arbeitsmöglichkeiten finden, die sie brauchen. Noch Schlimmeres bereitet sich auf den Schulen vor: In wenigen Jahren wird man, wenn nichts geschieht, die schulpflichtigen Kinder wieder nach Hause schicken müssen, weil es für sie weder Lehrer noch Klassenräume gibt. Es steht uns ein Bildungsnotstand bevor, den sich nur wenige vorstellen können.

Aus: G. Picht, *Die deutsche Bildungskatastrophe*. Freiburg: Walter, 1964.

Commentary

Germany's Educational Catastrophe — Die deutsche Bildungskatastrophe: possibly also *the catastrophe in Germany's education(al) system*. Neither versions are completely satisfactory, as catastrophe usually refers to an event, rather than a state such as the text describes. *The catastrophic state of education in Germany* would be a more accurate translation, but has the disadvantage of being rather long as a title.

1 **one of the essential foundations** — eines der tragenden Fundamente: not *fundamentals*, as this means 'basic principles' and thus avoids translating the concrete image of *tragende Fundamente*. Not *bases* (plural of *basis*), which is rarely used in its literal sense (see SOED, p. 151) and thus cannot convey the image. *Eine tragende Mauer* is a supporting or sustaining wall, but neither *supporting* nor *sustaining* collocate with *foundation*, which is felt to be *per se* supporting. A main quality of *a supporting wall* or *a foundation* is that it is necessary, or essential. We have chosen *essential* as a translation since it implies the 'necessary' aspect of a foundation, and at the same time reinforces the idea of something 'basic' in foundation. It would also be possible to transpose adjective and noun and translate *tragende Fundamente* as *fundamental supports*.

1 **every** — jedes: *each* here would be wrong, since *each* applies to one of a clearly limited number.

1 **educational system** — Bildungswesen: also *education system* or *system of education*.

2 **should** — müßte: see Leech, p. 95, on this use of *should*.

2 **the Germans** — die Deutschen: the almost colloquial *nobody should know*

countries together with Yugoslavia, Ireland and Portugal. Young scientists are
15 emigrating by the thousand because they no longer find the openings they
need at home. Even worse is in store for the schools: in a few years, if
nothing happens, the children of school-age will have to be sent back home
because there are neither teachers nor classrooms for them. We are facing a
state of emergency in education which only few can imagine.

    this ... is stylistically better followed by *the Germans* than by the more formal phrase *the German nation/people*.
2 **rise** — Aufstieg: also *ascent*.
3 **circle** — Kreis: also *group, ranks*.
3 **was founded on** — wurde ... durch ... begründet: also *found its roots in, had its roots in.* Also *the foundation of Germany's rise ... was given/provided by the expansion ...; the expansion ... gave/provided the foundation for Germany's rise ...*
3 **expansion** — Ausbau: also *extension, development,* although neither of these convey development in every direction, as *expansion* does.
4 **up to** — bis zum: also *until. Till* usually occurs in the spoken language, and is out of place here.
5 **position** — Stellung: also *status*.
5 **its economic prosperity** — seine wirtschaftliche Blüte: also *the flourishing of its economy,* or, transposing adjective and noun, *its flourishing economy*. Note the difference between *economic* and *economical, economic* referring to economics or the economy of a country, and *economical* meaning thrifty or saving. As it is also possible to use the feminine possessive adjective when referring to countries (and sometimes towns) *its* can be replaced by *her* here.
5 **the growth of its industry** — die Entfaltung seiner Industrie: also *its industrial growth. Development* and *expansion* are possible, too, the choice depending on avoiding what was already used to translate *Ausbau* above.
6 **on its then modern school-system** — auf seinem damals modernen Schulsystem: it is also possible to render *damals* in a relative clause as

follows: *on its school-system, which was at that time modern,* or, more idiomatically, *which was modern for its time.*

7 **had gained world-wide renown** — Weltgeltung erlangt hatte: other possibilities — *which had achieved world-wide acknowledgement/an international reputation, which was held in world-wide esteem.* Get/got, so often used in the spoken language, is best avoided in this kind of text.

7 **we are still drawing** — wir zehren bis heute: here the choice of tense and adverb are closely linked. If we translate *bis heute* as *still* we must use the Present Progressive (i.e. the process started in the past continues through the present into the future), but if we translate it as *until now* we must use the Perfect Progressive *we have been drawing... until now* (i.e. the process has occupied a period of time starting in the past and continuing up to the present moment).

8 **leaders** — Führungsschicht: although the phrase *ruling classes* exists, the collocation *leading classes* sounds extremely unusual. The leaders may constitute a group, but not a social class. It is therefore possible, though rather long, to say *the members of the leading economic and political groups.* Management is impossible, as although it might be used in an economic context, it cannot be used in a political context.

10 **the men** — die Kräfte: neither *forces* nor *powers* can be used in this sense.

10 **on whom ... depend** — die ... tragen: must be paraphrased. Also possible *who today make the decisions in ..., who today bear the responsibility for ..., who today take the lead in ...*

11 **were intellectually shaped** — verdanken ihre geistige Formung: also *formed/moulded.* Also possible *owe their intellectual shaping.*

11 **Weimar Period** — Weimarer Zeit: also *Weimar Republic/Era,* but not *Time.*

12 **has been exhausted** — ist ... verbraucht: also *spent, used up.* It is possible here to use the Present form *is exhausted.*

12 **statistics** — Statistik: *statistics* can also be the subject of the sentence — *comparative statistics on education show/reveal that the Federal Republic ...* Note that *statistics* is both the singular and the plural form of the word, and in the sense of 'numbers/data' is plural, hence *statistics ... show.*

13 **ranges at the lower end** — steht am unteren Ende: *range* is used here in the sense of occupying a position, and occurs frequently in this meaning in the context of position on a scale, in a list, in statistics, etc. *Rank* could also

be used here, but *stand* is impossible. A possible variant: *occupies a position at the lower end.*
14 **together with** — neben: also *next to, side by side with, beside, in the company of.*
14 **scientists** — Wissenschaftler: the reference is, presumably, to men doing research in the field of natural and physical science. *Scholar* would here imply men doing research in the field of the arts.
14 **are emigrating** — wandern aus: both the Present Progressive and the Present Simple give grammatically correct sentences, but sentences with slightly different meanings. The use of the Present Simple implies a permanent state, which is not quite compatible with *no longer,* and simply states a fact. The use of the Present Progressive, on the other hand, implies that this state of affairs is temporary, is of fairly recent origin, is actually going on at the time of writing, and is likely to continue. This is entirely compatible with *no longer* (implying the beginning of the action), and the urgency of what the author is saying.
15 **by the thousand** — zu Tausenden: also *in thousands, in their thousands,* but not **by thousands.*
15 **no longer** — nicht mehr: a verb preceded by *no longer* does not require the auxiliary *do,* thus versions such as **they do no longer find* are unacceptable.
15 **openings** — Arbeitsmöglichkeiten: if *Arbeitsmöglichkeiten* is interpreted as meaning actual posts, then *opportunities of employment* could be used. If it is interpreted as the type or conditions of work involved in a post rather than the post itself, then *working facilities* could be used. We have chosen *openings,* as it implies both — posts, together with good prospects.
16 **at home** — in ihrem Vaterland: also *in their native country.*
16 **is in store for** — bereitet sich vor: also *is to come*; not *is progressing, is preparing itself.*
17 **happens** — geschieht: also *is done.*
17 **the children of school-age** — die schulpflichtigen Kinder: also *the school-age children,* or simply, *the school-children.*
18 **because there are** — weil es gibt: also *because there will be.*
18 **we are facing** — es steht uns bevor: also *a state of emergency ... is awaiting us/is imminent/is approaching; we are facing a crisis.*

6. Die Entstehung des Romans

Die Entstehungsgeschichte des Romans ist wiederholt untersucht worden; man hat die sich mit der bürgerlichen Gesellschaft herausbildenden Bedingungen — den Auseinanderfall von gesellschaftlichem und privatem Leben, die Vereinzelung des Menschen, den Individualismus, die neue Naturwissenschaft und Erfahrungsphilosophie, den Journalismus, das neue, erweiterte Lesepublikum, usw. — als wichtige Voraussetzungen der Romanform erkannt. Damit sind gewiß entscheidende gesellschafts- und ideengeschichtliche Wandlungen berücksichtigt worden, die erstmalig die erzählerische Gestaltung eines gänzlich auf sich gestellten, kaufmännischen Helden wie Robinson ermöglichten. Welches aber sind die konkreten künstlerischen Formen, in denen sich der Entstehungsprozeß der neuen Gattung vollzog? Warum und auf welche Weise führten diese historischen Voraussetzungen gerade zu einer *künstlerisch* überlegenen Gestaltung von Wirklichkeit, zu einem qualitativ neuen Realismus in der Literatur?

Diese Fragen harren noch immer einer befriedigenden Antwort. Und obwohl doch das Erzählwerk des Robinson-Dichters ein geradezu beispielhaftes Anschauungsmaterial bietet, hat die Defoe-Forschung diese Fragestellung in der Regel übergangen.

... Die tatsächlichen Beziehungen zwischen den historisch-sozialen Grundlagen und den künstlerischen Formen ihrer Widerspiegelung sind überhaupt selten konsequent erforscht worden. Der Zusammenhang zwischen dem gesellschaftlichen und kulturhistorischen *Inhalt* des Defoeschen Romans und seiner spezifischen erzählerischen *Formgebung* ist jedoch weit enger als von den Literaturkritikern dargestellt wird. Die Beziehungslosigkeit zwischen der literarhistorischen Rekonstruktion der Quellen, des Lebens, des „Milieus" usw. und der impressionistischen und ästhetizistischen Deutung des Kunstwerkes hat diese Tatsache verdunkelt. Die marxistische Forschung will diesen Zusammenhang erhellen, denn sie weiß, daß auch die künstlerische Form des Romans so wenig zeitlos ist, daß erst der lebendige Wirklichkeitsbezug das vermeintliche „Geheimnis" ihrer Wirkung erhellen kann.

Aus: R. Weimann, *Daniel Defoe. Eine Einführung in das Romanwerk.* Halle/Leipzig: VEB Max Niemeyer Verlag, 1962.

Commentary

1 **genesis** — Entstehungsgeschichte: also *origin*, possibly *development* or *rise*.
1 **examined** — untersucht: also *analyzed*, possibly *researched* (American

6. The Genesis of the Novel

The history of the genesis of the novel has been examined repeatedly. The conditions developing parallel to the rise of bourgeois society – the gulf between social and private life, the isolation of man, individualism, the new science and empiricism, journalism, the new, extended reading public – have been recognised to be important preconditions of the novel form. Crucial changes in society and the history of ideas which for the first time made possible the narrative creation of a totally self-reliant mercantile hero such as Robinson have thus indeed been taken into consideration. But what are the concrete artistic forms in which the development of the new genre took place? Why and how did these historical preconditions lead of all things to an *artistically* superior presentation of reality, to a qualitatively new realism in literature?

These questions are still awaiting a satisfactory answer. And although the 'Robinson' author's narrative presents a perfect example to illustrate this, Defoe scholarship has as a rule disregarded this line of research.

... The actual relationships between the social conditions of the time and the aesthetic forms in which they found their reflection have indeed rarely been the subject of systematic research. The connection between the social and cultural *content* of Defoe's novel and its specific narrative *form* is far narrower than is described by literary critics. The lack of connection between the historical reconstruction of sources, biography, milieu, etc., on the one hand, and the impressionistic and aestheticistic interpretation of the work of art on the other hand have obscured this fact. It is the intention of Marxist research to shed light on this connection in the knowledge that the aesthetic form of the novel is not timeless; indeed far from it, only the living connection to reality can illuminate the supposed secret of its effect.

English). Also *research has repeatedly been carried out into the genesis of...*

2 **gulf** — Auseinanderfall: also *separation, rift. Auseinanderfall* can express both a state and a process. If it is felt here to express a process, then *growing (the growing gulf/rift)* would need to be added. *Disintegration,* a common translation among the students, would imply here that both social life and private life were 'falling to pieces', rather than moving away from each other.
3 **isolation** — Vereinzelung: as in the previous item, if *Vereinzelung* is felt here to express a process, then *isolation* would need to be modified, for example, by *increasing.*
3 **individualism** — den Individualismus;
4 **journalism** — den Journalismus: zero article (abstract mass nouns, see Quirk et al., p. 153). *Science* (1. 4), however, is specified by *new,* and thus takes the definite article.
4 **have been recognised to be** — man hat ... als ... erkannt: also *recognised as, recognised as being.*
5 **crucial** — entscheidende: also *decisive* or, less strong, *significant.*
6 **in society and the history of ideas** — gesellschafts- und ideengeschichtliche: also *social and ideological (changes).* The choice of translation here is closely linked to the choice of translation of *entscheidend.* The repetition of the suffix *-al,* while acceptable in adjectives of the same rank (e.g. *social, philosophical and ideological changes*), is felt not to be particularly euphonious in adjectives of different rank, as in *crucial social and ideological changes,* where the phonological level suggests a rank similarity which is not matched on a semantic level. *Decisive* would in this case be a better translation for *entscheidend.*
6 **changes ... which** — Wandlungen ..., die: it would perhaps be possible to place the relative clause after the verb (*have been taken into consideration which* ...), but in English the relative clause, to avoid ambiguity, normally follows its antecedent as closely as possible.
8 **what** — welches: *what* seems preferable to *which* here. *Which* would suggest a selection or choice from some pre-existing limited number, whereas *what* seeks information of a defining nature, and does not suggest any fixed number (see Quirk et al., p. 216).
In the case of the pair of sentences
Which is your car?   What is your car?
the speaker of the first would be referring to a fixed number of cars, for example in a car-park, known to himself and the interlocutor, and his interlocutor might reply *It's the red one on the left,* thus singling out one car from a fixed number; the speaker of the second sentence, on the other

hand, would be seeking information about the car, for example about the kind or make, and the answer might be *It's a 1935 Bentley*.
Similarly, the question *Which are the concrete artistic forms...?* would seem to imply the pre-existence of some sort of list of artistic forms, and a selection from this list, whereas the question *What are the concrete artistic forms...?* seeks a naming or definiton of the forms.

9 **artistic** – künstlerischen: also *literary* or *aesthetic*.
11 **artistically** – künstlerisch;
11 **qualitatively** – qualitativ: note that the German forms *künstlerisch* and *qualitativ* modify *überlegenen* and *neuen* respectively, and thus have an adverbial, not adjectival, function.
13 **are awaiting** – harren: here the Simple Present form would also be acceptable. The sentence would then have something of the flavour of an 'eternal truth' – a weighty pronouncement with a certain finality about it.
14 **the 'Robinson' author's narrative** – das Erzählwerk des Robinson-Dichters: also *the narrative of the author of 'Robinson'*, possibly *the narrative in 'Robinson Crusoe'*.
14 **a perfect example to illustrate this** – ein geradezu beispielhaftes Anschauungsmaterial: also *an illustration of an indeed exemplary nature*. *Virtually* as a translation of *geradezu* would probably be avoided here by many English-speakers (*virtually exemplary*) because of the close similarity between the endings [li] and [ləri].
15 **scholarship** – Forschung: also *research*, if this is not used later in the sentence. Also *Defoe scholars*.
15 **as a rule** – in der Regel: also *usually* or *on the whole*.
15 **disregarded** – übergangen: also *ignored, passed over, skimmed over*.
15 **line of research** – Fragestellung: other possible translations: *aspect* or *line of study/enquiry*.
16 **social conditions of the time** – historisch-sozialen Grundlagen: again the problem of the double adjective, here solved by the use of the prepositional phrase *of the time*. *Pertaining at the time* would be an acceptable variant. It might also be possible to translate *Grundlagen* as *basic conditions*, in which case the word-order would be *basic social conditions*. Also possible *the social background*.
17 **aesthetic** – künstlerischen: also *literary, artistic* (see above).
17 **in which they found their reflection** – ihrer Widerspiegelung: also contact clause *they were mirrored in*.
18 **the subject of systematic research** – konsequent erforscht worden: variants: *have rarely been subject/subjected to systematic research/study/examina-*

43

tion/scrutiny/investigation, have rarely been systematically studied/examined/investigated/scrutinized.
19 **content** — Inhalt: *content* here refers to some general meaning expressed in a text, whereas *contents* would suggest something enumerable, for example (and most frequent in this context) the *Inhaltsverzeichnis/Contents* or *Table of Contents,* or a summary of the details of a text.
19 **of Defoe's novel** — des Defoeschen Romans: also possible perhaps *of the Defoe novel.* There is no adjective form based on Defoe as there is, for example, on Shakespeare (*Shakespearian*) and Dickens (*Dickensian*). Note that these two adjectives not only mean 'by Shakespeare' and 'by Dickens' respectively, but can also mean 'in the manner of/having the characteristics of Shakespeare/Dickens'.
19 **specific** — spezifischen: also *particular.*
20 **narrower** — enger: also *closer.*
20 **than is described by literary critics** — als von den Literaturkritikern dargestellt wird: it is also possible to say *than literary critics describe it to be.*

---

7. Die Bedeutung des autobiographischen Schrifttums

Die Bedeutung des autobiographischen Schrifttums und die Aufgabe, es zum Gegenstand einer wissenschaftlichen Behandlung zu nehmen, sind seit der Epoche der Aufklärung in England, Frankreich und Deutschland von verschiedenen Seiten her erkannt worden. Schon die Humanisten waren durch das Interesse an ihren antiken Vorgängern oder Vorbildern in der Selbstdarstellung zuweilen zu einer objektiven Auffassung dieses Kulturphänomens, in menschlicher oder literarischer Betrachtung gelangt; im 18. Jahrhundert, dem die großen Selbstbiographien der Renaissance als eine geschlossene Produktion vorlagen, wuchs mit der Energie der inneren Erfahrung und der historischen Reflexion zugleich die Wertschätzung der Selbstbiographien. Man forderte und veranstaltete Sammlungen der Bekenntnisse merkwürdiger Männer, gab Überblicke über die bekannteren Werke, versuchte sie zu klassifizieren. Und bei diesen Bestrebungen, an denen Historiker, Philosophen und Dichter hohen, ja höchsten Ranges, Gibbon, Herder und Goethe beteiligt waren, die selber auch als Autobiographen hervorragten, traten verschiedene Gesichtspunkte für die Auffassung dieser Schriftengattung hervor. Der Wert solcher Lebensdokumente für die Welt- und Menschenkenntnis wurde anerkannt; man sah es als einen Vorzug an, daß

21 **on the one hand ... on the other hand** –: The items between which there is a connection are morphologically clearly marked in the German text. The English text, lacking a definite article marked for case, is not quite so unambiguous. The addition of *on the one hand ... on the other hand,* although by no means obligatory, helps to restore unambiguity.

23 **it is the intention of** — will: *wants to* expresses a desire rather than an intention, and is thus inappropriate here, the more so because *wants* usually occurs with a personal subject (in the meaning of *desires*). Other possibilities: *Marxist research seeks to/intends to/aims to.*

24 **in the knowledge that** — denn sie weiß: the translation *for it knows* is unsatisfactory, as *knows*, like *wants* (see above), normally occurs with a personal subject. If, however, *marxistische Forschung* is translated by *Marxist scholars*, then *sie weiß* can be translated by *they know*.

25 **is not timeless; indeed far from it** — so wenig zeitlos ist, daß: variant for *far from it* might be *on the contrary*. Possible, though rather involved and thus not very clear, *is so far from being timeless that ...*

---

7. The Significance of Autobiographical Literature

Since the Age of Enlightenment the significance of autobiographical literature and the task of making it the object of scientific research have been recognized in different quarters in England, France and Germany. Through their interest in their classical predecessors or models in autobiography the
5 humanists had occasionally achieved an objective conception of this cultural phenomenon, from a human or a literary point of view. For the 18th century the great autobiographies of the Renaissance existed as a complete corpus, and as the energy of inner experience and historical reflection increased, so did the valuation placed upon autobiographies. Collections of the confessions
10 of notable men were sought and arranged, surveys of the better-known works were produced and attempts were made to classify them. In the course of these efforts, in which historians, philosophers and poets of high, indeed of the highest rank — Gibbon, Herder and Goethe, themselves also eminent autobiographers — took part, different aspects emerged for the conception of
15 this literary form. It was recognized that such biographical documentation was of value for a knowledge of the world and of man. It was regarded as an advantage that lives were presented in all their minute yet often so characteristic detail, and the usefulness of this literature was stressed: it was

in ihnen die Lebensläufe mit all den kleinen, aber oft doch so charakteristischen Einzelheiten behandelt waren und betonte die Nützlichkeit dieser Schriften: sie sollten den Leser nicht bloß unterhalten, sondern ihn fördern und ihm behilflich sein, durch Belehrung oder durch Warnung.

Aus: G. Misch, *Geschichte der Autobiographie*, 4 Bde., Frankfurt: Schulte-Bulmke, 1949–1969.

Commentary

Significance – Bedeutung: a frequent mistake here was to translate *Bedeutung* by *meaning*. *Bedeutung* covers the semantic field 'meaning' – 'important meaning' – 'meaningful importance' – 'importance'. *Significance*, which contains the two elements 'importance' and 'meaning', roughly covers the central area of the range ('important meaning', 'meaningful importance'), the relative stress being determined by the context. *Bedeutung* in the present context would seem to cover the 'meaningful importance' – 'importance' end of the range. *Significance*, then, is a possible translation, as is *importance*, but *meaning*, although in certain contexts it could replace *significance*, is inappropriate here.

1 **literature** – Schrifttum: also *writing;* note that there is no definite article (see Quirk et al., p. 153).
2 **the task of** – die Aufgabe, ... zu: *the task to is unacceptable.
2 **object of ... research** – Gegenstand einer ... Behandlung: strictly speaking, *object of research* is a more precise translation here than *subject of research*. *Subject* in this context would imply the theme or topic of what is to be studied, whereas *Gegenstand* and *object* imply the actual material which is to be studied. Interestingly, SOED (p. 2058, III, 4b) gives a definition of *subject* (in the sense as in 'Children learn many subjects in school – French, History, Biology, etc.') as *object of study*.
2 **scientific** – wissenschaftlichen: this term, once restricted to use in the field of natural sciences, is being used with increasing frequency in the literary field. Also possible *scholarly, academic*.
2 **research** – Behandlung: also *study*.
2 **have been recognized** – sind erkannt worden: also *realized*. The Simple Past would be wrong here as the link from the past to the present (i.e. the time of writing) is clearly indicated in *since*.
3 **in different quarters** – von verschiedenen Seiten her: *by different groups of people* would also be possible.

intended not merely to entertain the reader but also to improve and aid him
20 by instruction or by warning.

4 **classical** — antiken: also *ancient;* possibly *antique,* which however is only used in this sense in a highly restricted and specialized literary context. It is most frequently used in association with old furniture, objets d'art, etc., and is only to be used with caution in the literary sense by the non-native-speaker.
4 **models** — Vorbildern: not *idols,* which would imply an unreasoned worship of the classical authors on the part of the humanists.
4 **autobiography** — Selbstdarstellung: possibly *self-portrayal.* Definitely not *self-portrait,* which is countable, and refers to a single pictorial or verbal representation. The collective *self-portraiture* might just be possible.
5 **the humanists** — schon die Humanisten: **already the humanists* is unacceptable. *Schon* in this structure and meaning cannot be translated without a rather lengthy paraphrase such as *as far back as the 16th century* or *as long ago as the 16th century* or *the humanists were the first to ...,* none of which are entirely satisfactory as they all lay greater emphasis than *schon.* It seems advisable, then, to omit translating *schon* altogether. In certain cases, where no direct translation is possible or where a paraphrase would give the unit of meaning far more prominence than it warrants, lexical items such as *schon, doch, einmal, noch,* etc. may be left untranslated. No general rule can be formulated here — each case must be judged on its own merits.
5 **had achieved** — waren gelangt: also *had reached, had arrived at. Gain* is not entirely satisfactory here. Whereas *gelangen* and *achieve* suggest obtaining as the successful end of a process involving effort on the part of the subject, *gain* does not imply the difficulty of the process or the effort involved.
5 **conception** — Auffassung: variants are *comprehension, understanding.*
6 **for the 18th century** — im 18. Jahrhundert: this sentence presented great difficulties to the students regarding the order of the phrases and clauses.

It is of course possible to retain the single sentence structure (*in the 18th century, when ..., as ..., so ...*). It seemed however preferable to render the one German sentence as two sentences conjoined by *and* in the English text. The suggested version has the advantage of avoiding a piling-up of phrases and clauses before the main clause, and also of avoiding the difficulty of translating *im 18. Jahrhundert, dem ... (when? to which? for which?)*.

7 **complete corpus** — geschlossene Produktion: also *corporate whole*, possibly *complete production*. Not *œuvre*, which refers to a work or the works of an individual author, or *opus*, which refers to a single piece of work.

8 **as ... so ...** — zugleich: the translation *the valuation placed on autobiography grew together with the energy of inner experience ...* does not necessarily imply that the energy of inner experience was also in the process of growing, and is thus unclear in its meaning. The following translations might be possible — *the valuation ... increased parallel to/in proportion to the increase in the energy ...* . Both *parallel to* and *in proportion to* imply that the growth took place on both sides, but both give slightly more information than *zugleich*. Hence the choice of *as ..., so ...*, which makes the relationship between valuation and energy clear without giving additional information.

9 **valuation** — Wertschätzung: *evaluation* is inappropriate here as it expresses the process of evaluing rather than the value arrived at (*valuation*).

9 **collections** — Sammlungen: also possibly *anthologies*, although *anthology* suggests a collection of shorter pieces of work from different authors or extracts from their work, which is not necessarily implied by the less specific *Sammlungen*.

9 **confessions** — Bekenntnisse: *memoirs* might just be possible here, but it lays more stress on events and the reactions of the author (probably a participant) to them, whereas *Bekenntnisse* and *confessions* stress the author's presentation of his own life, character and thoughts, rather than contemporary events.

10 **notable** — merkwürdig: also *remarkable, noteworthy*, possibly *brilliant*.

10 **were sought** — man forderte: also *were demanded*. For various English renderings of the German impersonal *man* structure, see Friederich, p. 116–119.

10 **arranged** — veranstaltete: also *organized, instigated*.

10 **surveys** — Überblicke: also possibly *outlines*. *Review* in this literary context (*reviews of the better-known works*) would necessarily have the meaning of 'pieces of literary criticism', which is inappropriate here.

11 **attempts were made** – versuchte: also *attempts were undertaken, (their classification) was attempted.* Not **their classification was tried.*
12 **efforts** – Bestrebungen: also *endeavours.*
12 **of high, indeed of the highest rank** – hohen, ja höchsten Ranges: the collocations *of the highest order* and *of the first order* exist and would be acceptable translations for *höchsten Ranges,* but neither allows for a translation of *hohen (Ranges),* as *of high order* is a very unusual collocation, and *first* does not allow the contrast between a basic form and a superlative form.
13 **themselves ...** – die selber ...: whereas in German the relative clause need not immediately follow its antecedent, the English relative clause is better placed close to its antecedent. This however would give us a relative clause within a relative clause, and a long and complex subject followed by a single word predicate *(participated).* This imbalance can be made rather more tolerable by reducing the second relative clause to a noun phrase in apposition.
13 **eminent autobiographers** – als Autobiographen hervorragten: also *acknowledged/excellent/distinguished/outstanding autobiographers* or *autobiographers of repute.*
14 **took part** – beteiligt waren: also *participated.*
14 **emerged** – traten hervor: variants: *were revealed, were brought forward, were brought to light.*
15 **literary form** – Schriftengattung: also *genre.*
15 **it was recognized that** – wurde anerkannt: it is of course also possible to construct the sentence similarly to the German – *the value of ... was recognized.*
15 **biographical documentation** – Lebensdokumente: also possible *biographical documents, records of life.*
16 **knowledge of man** – Menschenkenntnis: variants: *of mankind, of human nature.*
16 **it was regarded as** – man sah es als ... an: also *it was considered to be.*
17 **lives** – Lebensläufe: *curriculum vitae* corresponds to *Lebenslauf* only in certain circumstances, namely, when it refers to a formal written record of the important dates, events and stages in a man's life, written for example in connection with an application for a post, etc. Thus it is inappropriate here. *Career* is not possible as it stresses the public side of a man's life, for example, his progress in his profession, and is thus incompatible with *minute ... characteristic detail. Personal records* might be possible.

17 **in all their ... detail** — mit all den ... Einzelheiten: this is rather more idiomatic than *with all their ... details.*
17 **minute** — kleinen: variants: *tiny, trifling, minor. Small* is only possible in conjunction with the plural form *details.*
18 **usefulness** — Nützlichkeit: also *utility.*
18 **was stressed** — (man) betonte: also *was underlined, emphasized.* Also *it was emphasized how useful ...*

---

8. Analyse eines *comic strip* auf der Oberstufe

Die Existenz, der Einfluß, die Verbreitung von *comic strips* — besonders in der angelsächsischen Welt — läßt sich nicht leugnen. Die Zahlen sind widersprüchlich, aber das Leserpublikum der *comic strips* geht in die Millionen. Ziel einer Unterrichtsreihe über diese Art der Trivialliteratur muß der Versuch sein, den Schülern die Möglichkeit zu geben, den *comic strip* als Informations- und Kommunikationsmittel für Millionen von Menschen zu erkennen und ihnen die unter Umständen gefährliche Wirkung dieses Teils der Popkultur zu zeigen. Dazu gehört, daß sie die Techniken erkennen, mit denen der *comic*-Zeichner sein Publikum fesselt, daß ihnen die Vorurteile und Stereotypen, die sich in den *strips* finden, bewußt gemacht werden.

Aus diesen Andeutungen geht hervor, wie vielseitig und ausbaufähig das Thema *comic strip* für den Englischunterricht und darüber hinaus für die allgemeine Erziehung sein kann, die bei unserem auf Faktenwissen ausgerichteten Unterricht oft zu kurz kommt. Es ist meines Erachtens falsch, den Schülern eine Welt anspruchsvoller *short stories,* Dramen und Essays im Unterricht darzubieten und an populären Literaturformen vorbeizugehen. Der Schüler muß lernen, wertvolle Texte von wertlosen zu unterscheiden, Informationen kritisch aufzunehmen und zu analysieren. Er erhält Bewertungsmaßstäbe, die es ihm ermöglichen, auch minderwertige bzw. ausgesprochen schlechte Literatur zu beurteilen. Der Wert des Themas für den Englischunterricht speziell liegt darin, daß der Schüler an diesem Ausschnitt aus der Popkultur lernt, Bilder sprachlich zu bewältigen. Detaillierte Bildbeschreibung, die zur Analyse der Bildinhalte notwendig ist, kann auch vom weniger sprachgewandten Schüler der Klassen 12 und 13 geleistet werden und integriert damit den Schüler, der sich von anspruchsvolleren literarischen Interpretationen ausgeschlossen fühlen mag, in den Unterricht.

Aus: U. Vater, *Batman — Wanted for Murder,* in: *Der fremdsprachliche Unterricht* 4/1972. Stuttgart: Ernst Klett, 1972.

19 **not merely ... but also** — nicht bloß ..., sondern: note the position of *not merely* and *but also*, immediately preceding *to entertain* and *to improve*, the two parallel parts of the opposition. *Not only* is also possible. Note also that in the German opposition *nicht nur ..., sondern (auch)* the *auch* is optional; in English the *also (not only ... but also)* is nearly always present.
19 **improve and aid** — fördern und behilflich sein: also *advance/educate and help*.

---

8. Analysis of a Comic Strip with Senior Classes

The existence, influence and widespread distribution of comic strips — particularly in the English-speaking world — is undeniable. The figures are contradictory, but comic strip readership runs into millions. The aim of a teaching project on trivial literature of this nature must be the attempt to
5 provide pupils with the opportunity to recognize the comic strip as a medium of information and communication for millions of people, and to demonstrate to the pupils the potentially dangerous effect of this section of pop-culture. This involves their recognizing the techniques the comic strip artist uses to grip the attention of his public, and their being made aware of
10 the prejudices and stereotypes which are to be found in the strips.

It follows from these remarks how many-sided and exploitable the comic strip is as a subject in English teaching and beyond that in the pupils' general education, which in our fact-orientated teaching is often neglected. In my opinion, it is wrong to confront the pupil in class with a world of demanding
15 short stories, plays and essays, and to pass over popular literary forms. The pupil has to learn to distinguish between texts of literary value and worthless texts, to take in information critically and to analyse it. He receives criteria which make it possible for him to evaluate literature of inferior quality and actual trash as well. The value of this subject for English teaching in particular
20 lies in the pupil's learning from this section of pop-culture to deal with pictures verbally. The detailed description of a picture which is necessary for the analysis of the content of the picture can be managed, too, by the linguistically less able pupil in classes 12 and 13, and thus integrates into the lesson the pupil who may feel excluded from more exacting literary
25 interpretations.

Commentary

with Senior Classes — auf der Oberstufe: here there are several other possible translations, such as *with senior forms, with older pupils, with advanced classes*, all of which are neutral in that they could be used to refer to any school-system. Variants such as *in the sixth-form, in sixth-form work, in A-level classes, in the upper school*, are also acceptable, but it should be noted that they refer specifically to the English school-system. A translation involving *secondary* is inappropriate as *secondary* applies to all education between the ages of 11 and 18.

1 **widespread distribution** — Verbreitung: *distribution* in itself carries no component of meaning giving information about the nature of the distribution — wide, scattered, narrow, etc. — whereas *Verbreitung* in this context would suggest a large rather than a small distribution, hence the addition in the English text of the modifier *widespread*. Also *circulation* as a variant for *distribution*. *Spreading* gives information about a process which is taking place. This is more information than the German text gives, and is thus inappropriate.

2 **English-speaking world** — angelsächsischen Welt: the translation *Anglo-Saxon world*, while not absolutely wrong, is rather odd in this context, as *Anglo-Saxon* has mainly historical connotations for the English-speaker, and even if the British English-speaker were to associate *Anglo-Saxon* in a metaphorical sense with himself, it is doubtful whether this association would include American English-speakers. The author of this text, however, presumably wished to include the American scene.

2 **is undeniable** — läßt sich nicht leugnen: also *is not to be denied, cannot be denied, is beyond dispute*. This is a good example of a case where both the singular and the plural forms *is* and *are* are acceptable. If the subject is felt to be a unit (the existence, influence and widespread distribution = one fact, which is not to be denied), the singular form can be used. If each noun were preceded by its own determiner (the existence, the influence, etc.), the subject would probably be regarded as plural, and *are* would be used.

2 **the figures** — die Zahlen: also *numbers, statistics*. Note that *statistics* in its meaning as a field of study behaves as a singular noun, whereas *statistics* in the sense of collections of numerical data behaves as a plural noun.

2 **are contradictory** — sind widersprüchlich: also *contradict each other*. Not *controversial*. It certainly follows that if figures are contradictory, then they are likely to be subject to dispute, i.e. to be controversial, but the fact remains that the German text does not make this logical step, and

therefore *controversial* is not an exact rendering of the meaning of the German text.
3 **readership** — Leserpublikum: also *reading public*. Also *the number of comic strip readers, the number of people who read comic strips*. Note that vocabulary problems can sometimes be circumvented by an analytic rendering.
3 **runs into millions** — geht in die Millionen: variants: *amounts to millions, numbers millions, can be measured in millions*. *Goes up to millions* is rather unidiomatic.
4 **teaching project** — Unterrichtsreihe: also *teaching sequence, sequence/series of lessons*. *Row* is inappropriate.
4 **on** — über: also *about*.
4 **trivial literature of this nature** — diese Art der Trivialliteratur: also *this sort of/this kind of trivial literature*. Also ... *popular literature*.
4 **must be** — muß ... sein: rather more idiomatic *can only be*.
5 **opportunity to recognize** — die Möglichkeit ... zu erkennen: also *of recognizing*. *Realize* is possible as a variant for *recognize*. The constructions *realize/recognize the comic strip to be, realize/recognize that the comic strip is,* are acceptable, but **realize the comic strip as,* a common mistake, is unacceptable.
5 **a medium of information ...** — Informations- ...mittel: this can also be translated as *an information and communication medium serving millions*.
7 **the potentially dangerous effect** — die unter Umständen gefährliche Wirkung: the translation of *unter Umständen* as *under certain circumstances* is perfectly correct, but difficult to fit into the sentence without lengthening it. Possible would be *the effect of ..., which under certain circumstances can be dangerous*.
7 **of this section** — dieses Teils: also *of this part/area*.
8 **of pop-culture** — der Popkultur: note the zero determiner in the English, as *pop-culture* is here unspecified. In the phrase *der Popkultur des 20. Jahrhunderts* pop-culture is specified and the translation would be *of the pop-culture of the 20th century*. Note however that if *des 20. Jahrhunderts* is translated as *in the 20th century*, then the degree of specification is not so great, and the translation would be *of pop-culture in the 20th century* (i.e. zero determiner).
8 **this involves** — dazu gehört: also possibly *includes*. Note the use of the gerund after these two verbs. *This involves that they recognize ...* sounds rather stilted.
8 **comic strip artist** — *comic*-Zeichner: also *cartoonist*. The fact that native

speakers disagree in their interpretation of *comic, comic strip, strip cartoon* and *cartoon* shows that this semantic field is at present in a state of flux. For this reason we have left *comic strip* throughout the text, although we personally have the feeling that the author is perhaps referring to a comic (complete story or stories, told in drawings, in magazine form) rather than what for us is a comic strip (story told in a row of drawings, very often in serial form, in a newspaper).

8 **the techniques (he) uses to grip** – die Techniken ..., mit denen (er) fesselt: also, of course, *the techniques with which/by means of which he grips ...* Variants for *grip the attention* are *fascinate, enthrall, captivate.*

10 **which are to be found** – die sich finden: also *which can be found*, or, simply, *to be found.*

11 **it follows from these remarks** – aus diesen Andeutungen geht hervor: other possible translations: *these remarks will have made it clear, it can be seen from these remarks, these remarks reveal.*

11 **many-sided** – vielseitig: *manifold,* meaning 'many and varied', normally collocates with a plural noun, e.g. *manifold aspects;* thus it is inappropriate as a modifier of *subject. Versatile* was a common translation, but is also inappropriate. *Versatile,* which normally collocates with a person or a personal quality, has an active meaning ('able to do many things') rather than the passive meaning 'able to have many things done to it', which is implied by the German text.

11 **exploitable** – ausbaufähig: this, understandably, caused the students a great deal of difficulty, this use of *exploit* as a technical term from the field of foreign language teaching being unknown to them. It would have been possible to avoid the pitfalls in *wie vielseitig und ausbaufähig* by an analytic paraphrase in the following manner – *how many (different) aspects and possibilities for further development the comic strip offers ...*

12 **subject** – Thema: also *theme* or *topic.* Alternative version: *what a many-sided and exploitable subject the comic strip is ...*

12 **in English teaching** – für den Englischunterricht: also *in English lessons, in the teaching of English.*

12 **beyond that** – darüber hinaus: also *furthermore, in addition.*

12 **general education** – die allgemeine Erziehung: not *common education,* as this suggests education which all children receive rather than education which is not directly related to a specific subject.

13 **in our fact-orientated teaching** – bei unserem auf Faktenwissen ausgerichteten Unterricht: also ... *knowledge-orientated* ... It is difficult to translate this phrase without going into lengthy paraphrase. Both versions have the

disadvantage that neither completely renders the German *Faktenwissen*, but the advantage of brevity. However, it could be argued that *fact-orientated* necessarily implies '*knowledge* of facts' and *knowledge-orientated* necessarily implies 'knowledge of *facts*'. **Knowledge of facts-orientated* is unacceptable. Alternative, lengthier translations would involve a catenation of relative clauses ... *which is often neglected in our teaching, which is orientated towards* ... This is stylistically unsatisfactory. A participle construction ... *in our teaching, orientated as it is towards factual knowledge/a knowledge of facts* might be a possible solution.

13 **is often neglected** — oft zu kurz kommt: variants: *is often disregarded/underrepresented, often plays a minor part.*
14 **in class** — im Unterricht: also *in the classroom, in his lessons.*
14 **demanding** — anspruchsvoller: also *difficult,* possibly *high standard.*
15 **to pass over** — vorbeizugehen: variants: *to pass by, not to deal with, to disregard, to neglect, to omit, to miss out, to leave out.*
16 **has to** — muß: both *has to* and *must* are acceptable here. However there is a slight shift in emphasis, which the students should be aware of. Where *must* and *have to* express obligation, *must* expresses obligation imposed by the speaker, and *has to* expresses obligation imposed from some other source. Thus here the use of *must* would imply that it is the speaker's opinion that it is necessary for the pupil to learn to distinguish ... etc., whereas the use of *has to* would express that the speaker thinks the pupil to be under some sort of universally imposed obligation or necessity (see Leech, p. 71–73).
16 **to distinguish** — zu unterscheiden: also *to differentiate, to make a distinction,* possibly *to make a difference.*
16 **of literary value ... worthless** — wertvolle ... wertlosen: *valuable,* while not wrong, is not totally satisfactory, as *valuable texts* seems to suggest 'texts worth a great deal of money'. Hence our inclusion of *literary*. Many students perceived this, but then went on to make the frequent bad mistake of confusing the [ri] ending (possibly reinforced by the initial [l]) with the adverbial [li] morpheme, and thus assuming *literary* to have an adverbial function. They produced **literary valuable texts*, which is totally unacceptable. Other students confused *literary* and *literal*, and produced *literally valuable*, which is grammatically acceptable, but translates *buchstäblich wertvoll* rather than *(literarisch) wertvoll.* Other alternative: *texts which are valuable from a literary point of view.* The adverb *literarily* exists theoretically but is virtually never used.
17 **to take in** — aufzunehmen: also *to assimilate.*

17 **information** – Informationen: note that *information* in English is a mass noun, and as such has no plural form.
17 **criteria** – Bewertungsmaßstäbe: also *(a set of) standards*. Note that a plural form **criterions* does not exist.
18 **which make it possible for him** – die es ihm ermöglichen: variants: *which enable him, thus becoming able to*.
18 **literature of inferior quality** – minderwertige ... Literatur: also *inferior literature, literature of lesser/minor value*.
18 **and** – bzw.: also *or*. *Respectively*, which is totally inappropriate here, is a good example of interference from the German *respektive* as a synonym for *beziehungsweise*.
19 **actual trash** – ausgesprochen schlechte Literatur: variants: *real rubbish, absolute rubbish, really poor literature*.
19 **in particular** – speziell: note the position. *Speziell* modifies *English teaching* and must therefore be positioned next to it, and not after the verb.

---

9. Ein Sowjet-Journalist über den amerikanischen Lebensstil (1)

Alle Amerikaner, ohne Ausnahme, bemühen sich, immer zu lächeln. Selbst ein Räuber, der einem Bank-Kassierer den Revolver auf die Brust setzt, lächelt zuerst und verlangt dann, ihm das ganze Bargeld in einen Hut zu werfen. Der Bankangestellte lächelt auch, tritt aber zugleich unbemerkt auf den Alarmknopf unter dem Schalter. Einige sind der Ansicht, daß der bekannte Ausspruch „Jeder Amerikaner kann Präsident werden" nicht ganz richtig ist. Nach ihrer Meinung müßte es heißen: „Jeder Amerikaner, der lachen kann, kann Präsident werden."

Amerikaner lächeln mühelos, ohne die geringste Anstrengung und auch völlig mechanisch, so als würden sie es immer tun. Das gilt auch für die Angewohnheit der amerikanischen Männer, immer ihre Hände in die Taschen zu stecken. Und auch für die Amerikanerinnen, die beim Sprechen so viel wie möglich ihre Zähne zeigen. Da sie praktisch veranlagte Menschen sind und vor allem die hohen Arztkosten gut kennen, achten sie mit allen Mitteln auf ihre Gesundheit. Eines dieser Mittel ist das Lächeln. Ich habe aber auch viele Menschen gesehen, bei denen nicht nur das Lachen, sondern selbst das elementarste menschliche Lächeln im Kampf gegen die ewige Armut und Verzweiflung erloschen war. Lachen und Tränen sowie Armut und Wohlstand gehören in Amerika zusammen wie Zwillinge.

Aus: *Ein Sowjet-Journalist über den amerikanischen Lebensstil*, in: *Der Spiegel* 15/1967.

20 **lies in the pupil's learning ...** – liegt darin, daß der Schüler ... lernt: alternatives: *lies in the fact that the pupil learns ..., is that the pupil learns ...*
20 **to deal with** – zu bewältigen: also, possibly, *to cope with* or *to express the content of,* although the latter, by being more specific, does not transmit the range of possibilities in *bewältigen*.
23 **linguistically less able pupil** – weniger sprachgewandten Schüler: variants: *less eloquent/gifted pupil, pupil less capable of expressing himself, pupil less able to express himself, pupil less skilful in the use of language.*
23 **classes 12 and 13** – Klassen 12 und 13: variant: *12th and 13th grades/classes.* If *Oberstufe* (see above) has been translated by a term specific to the English school-system, then *Klassen 12 und 13* must be translated by a concordant term, for example, *sixth-forms.*
24 **excluded from** – von ... ausgeschlossen: also *not up to, not able to cope with.*
24 **more exacting ... interpretations** – anspruchsvolleren ... Interpretationen: also *more ambitious ... interpretations, interpretations on a higher intellectual level.*

---

9. A Soviet Journalist on the American Way of Life (1)

All Americans, without exception, take great pains always to be smiling. Even a bank-robber holding a revolver at a cashier's chest smiles first and then orders him to throw all the cash into a hat. The bank-clerk smiles, too, but at the same time steps unnoticed on the alarm button beneath the counter.
5 Some people are of the opinion that the well-known saying 'Every American can become President' isn't quite true. In their opinion it should run 'Every American who can laugh can become President'.

Americans smile easily, without the least effort, and completely mechanically, as if they were always doing so. The same can be said of the
10 habit American men have of always sticking their hands into their pockets. And it also goes for American women, who show their teeth as much as possible when they speak. Being practical-minded and above all well aware of the high fees doctors charge, they take care of their health by every possible means. One of these means is smiling. Yet I saw many people in whom not
15 only laughter but even the most basic human smile had been extinguished in the battle against eternal poverty and despair. Laughter and tears as well as poverty and prosperity belong together in America like twins.

Commentary

on − über: *about* is possible if the title is expanded to *A Soviet Journalist talking/writing about*... This is rather long-winded, though. *On* is conventionally used in titles, indicating the theme of an article, when there is no verb present to influence the choice of preposition.

1 **take great pains** − bemühen sich: also *are at pains, try, endeavour, make an effort.*

1 **always to be smiling** − immer zu lächeln: rather more idiomatically *always to have a smile on their faces, to have a permanent smile on their faces.* The Simple Infinitive *always to smile* could replace the Progressive Infinitive here, but with a slight change of meaning. Whereas *to smile* expresses a single action, *to be smiling* stretches the action into something more resembling a state (see Leech, p. 15). Thus the Simple Infinitive here expresses 'always to smile whenever they meet anyone' and the Progressive Infinitive expresses 'always to be in a state of smiling', 'to have a permanent smile on their faces'.

To keep smiling is problematical, as this phrase has become a semantic unit different from the sum of its parts with the meaning of 'not allowing oneself to become despondent in the face of difficulties', and thus has inappropriate connotations here. However, in the presence of an adverb, e.g. *to keep permanently smiling* or *to keep smiling all the time*, the parts *keep* and *smiling* do not coalesce to express a new meaning, but retain their old meanings parallel to *keep running, keep talking*, etc. Either of these two versions, then, is possible here.

2 **bank-robber** − Räuber: also possibly *bank-raider*. Not simply *robber.*

2 **holding a revolver at a cashier's chest** − der einem Bank-Kassierer den Revolver auf die Brust setzt: a relative clause (*who is holding*...) is possible but not necessary. Also possible *holding a cashier at gun-point, holding up a cashier*, or *holding a revolver to a cashier's chest.*

2 **cashier** − Bank-Kassierer: also *teller; bank-cashier* is possible, but the repetition of *bank* is not necessary.

3 **orders him to throw** − verlangt ... zu werfen: the translation of *verlangt* is the source of a relatively large number of mistakes on the part of the German student, whereby the syntactic patterns following *command* and *demand* are confused. Correct would be here *commands him to throw*... or *demands that he throw* (Pres. Subj.)/*should throw*. Not *demands to throw.*

3 **all the cash** − das ganze Bargeld: *the whole cash* seems in this context unacceptable, but it is difficult to explain why. Whereas *he ate the whole loaf* (countable concrete noun), *he has been eating the whole day*

(countable abstract noun), *he fixed his whole attention on eating* (mass abstract noun) are all acceptable, *he ate the whole bread* (mass concrete noun) seems incongruous or at best possible in colloquial speech, where, however, *the whole of the bread* would be much more likely. It would seem, then, that *whole* in the phrase *the whole + N* collocates with countable concrete and countable abstract nouns, and with mass abstract nouns, but only rarely with mass concrete nouns. *Ready money* as a variant for *cash* would be rather inappropriate here as this usually refers to the money an individual has on him, or can get at easily, and implies a smaller sum than the amount a bank would have.

4 **steps** — tritt: this version has the advantage of not introducing yet another prepositional phrase into the sentence. Also possible *pushes/presses (the alarm button beneath the counter) with his foot, presses his foot on ...*

4 **unnoticed** — unbemerkt: can also immediately precede *steps*. *Without being noticed* is also possible in either of these positions. *Unobtrusively* would refer to the way in which the cashier acted, rather than the fact of his not being seen (*unbemerkt*), but as the effect is the same, it is probably permissible as a translation here.

4 **alarm button** — Alarmknopf: variants: *emergency button/bell.*
4 **beneath** — unter: also *under, below.*
4 **counter** — Schalter: not *desk.* Note that *Schalter* has various equivalents in English according to where it is, e.g. *counter* in a bank, *box-office* in a theatre, *ticket-office, booking-office* in a station.
5 **are of the opinion** — sind der Ansicht: also *maintain, think.*
5 **well-known** — bekannte: it is a very frequent mistake to translate *bekannt* in this context with *known*. Note that the comparative and superlative forms corresponding to *bekannter, -est* are *better-known* and *best-known.*
5 **saying** — Ausspruch: *slogan, watchword, proverb, adage* and *motto* are all inappropriate here. Briefly, a *slogan*, or *watchword*, is a fairly short phrase or sentence used by a group of people, e.g. a political party, to represent their policy (e.g. 'Homes for All'). A *proverb*, or *adage*, is a traditional saying (e.g. 'Too many cooks spoil the broth'). A *motto* is a phrase or sentence, possibly a proverb, often in Latin, which an individual, a family, a group or an institution take as representative of the behaviour they aspire to, or their philosophy of life, e.g. 'Never say die'.
5 **every American** — jeder Amerikaner: not *each.* The main difference between *each* and *every* is that *each* always refers to one of a fixed or relatively limited number whereas *every* tends towards generality. If we paraphrase the meaning of *each* and *every* as 'all the single items or elements in a

6 **in their opinion** — nach ihrer Meinung: not *after their opinion*. Not *according to their opinion*, possibly *according to them*.
6 **should** — müßte: also *ought to*.
8 **without the least effort** — ohne die geringste Anstrengung: also *without the slightest effort*, or *effortlessly*, although the use of this would result in a chain of four adverbs ending in [li] (*easily, effortlessly* and *completely mechanically*) which is not particularly euphonious. A common mistake was the omission of the adverb ending in *completely mechanically*.
9 **as if** — so als: not *so as, *so as if.
9 **they were always doing so** — würden sie es immer tun: also *they were always doing it*.
9 **the same can be said** — das gilt auch: variants: *the same applies to, the same is true of, the same holds good for*.
10 **the habit ... of sticking their hands ...** — die Angewohnheit ..., ihre Hände .. zu stecken: here students frequently confused the two structures illustrated in *they have the habit of sticking their hands into their pockets* and *it is their habit to stick their hands into their pockets*, and produced the unacceptable structure **the habit American men have to stick ...* Habit followed by *to + inf.* is only used in an impersonal construction with the anticipatory subject *it*, as in *it is their habit to stick ...* whereby *to stick ...* can be identified as a postponed subject (see Quirk et al., p. 963). This can be illustrated by the sentence *to stick his hands into his pockets is his habit*, where *to stick ...* occupies the normal subject position. A variant for *stick* is *put*.
11 **American women, who** — die Amerikanerinnen, die: generic (as opposed to specific) reference (see Quirk et al., p. 153), therefore zero determiner. The comma is necessary as it indicates that the relative clause is non-defining. The author wishes to imply that *all* American women show their teeth when smiling. The omission of the comma would alter the meaning and the relative clause would have the function of defining *a particular group* of American women who have this habit.
12 **when they speak** — beim Sprechen: also *when speaking*.

12 **being practical-minded** – da sie praktisch veranlagte Menschen sind: also *being practically-minded, being practical people by nature, being practical in their outlook, as they are practical-minded people;* possibly *being pragmatists*.
12 **above all** – vor allem: not **before all*.
12 **... well aware of** – gut kennen: also *well aware how high ... are, well know how high ... are*.
13 **the high fees doctors charge** – die hohen Arztkosten: also *the high charges for medical treatment, high doctors' bills*. *Exorbitant* is possible as a variant for *high*, although it is of course much stronger. *Price* as a variant for *charge* or *fee* is inappropriate here as it usually refers to the amount an object, rather than a service, costs.
13 **take care of** – achten ... auf: also *look after*.
13 **by every possible means** – mit allen Mitteln: the phrase *by all means* does of course exist, but it is used as a fixed expression to give the affirmative answer to a request for permission to do something, as in *May I ...? By all means/of course/go ahead, I've no objection*, and thus is totally inappropriate here. Note that the singular and plural forms of *means* in this meaning are identical.
14 **smiling** – das Lächeln: also *the smile*.
14 **I saw** – ich habe gesehen: the use of the Simple Past is justified here by the fact that the author is no longer in New York, and thus the period of time referred to was completed in the past. However, the Present Perfect could also be used here, implying 'in the course of the years up to the present moment'.
14 **not only ... but even** – nicht nur ..., sondern selbst: note that these immediately precede the two parallel parts of the opposition, in this case the noun phrases centred on *laughter* and *smile*. A translation such as *laughter not only disappeared* is wrong in this context, as it raises the expectation of another verb, e.g. *but also died*.
15 **had been extinguished** – erloschen war: variants: *had died, had disappeared, had vanished, had been snuffed out*.
16 **in the battle** – im Kampf: also *in the fight, in the struggle*.
16 **despair** – Verzweiflung: also *hopelessness*.
17 **prosperity** – Wohlstand: also *affluence, wealth*. Not *welfare*.

10. Ein Sowjet-Journalist über den amerikanischen Lebensstil (2)

Sei es beim Essen, bei einer Tasse Kaffee oder auf einem Bankett, drei Gesprächsthemen können die Amerikaner nie vermeiden: ihre Autos, ihre Verdauung und ihre Schlaflosigkeit.

Vor ihren Häusern legen die Amerikaner keine Gärten an. Sie säen einen dichten Rasen, den sie einmal in der Woche mähen und sechsmal wöchentlich sprengen. In Amerika werden Häuser nur selten umzäunt. Lediglich sehr teure Villen, alte Parkanlagen, Gefängnisse und Irrenanstalten sind von hohen Zäunen mit starken Eisentoren umgeben ...

Amerikaner denken äußerst praktisch und wirtschaftlich. Während der Mann im Büro nach Gehaltserhöhungen strebt, ist seine Frau ständig bemüht, die Haushaltungskosten zu senken. Die Frauen durchblättern häufig die Zeitungen, um zu erfahren, welche Waren besonders günstig verkauft werden, damit sie sich abends beim Essen rühmen können, einen halben Dollar bei einem Paar Schuhe, 25 Cent bei einem Hemd, 40 Cent bei vier Flaschen italienischem Olivenöl und 60 Cent bei zwei Pfund Fleisch gespart zu haben.

Amerikaner trinken immer und überall Unmengen Kaffee. Wenn sie sich nicht damit aufputschen können, werden sie schnell mürrisch und gereizt und können nicht mehr arbeiten.

Während der drei Jahre, die ich in New York lebte, hat man mir kein einziges Mal ein verfaultes Ei, einen wurmstichigen Apfel oder ranzige Butter verkauft. Doch ich habe auch nie ein schmackhaftes frisches Ei gegessen oder eine Gurke oder eine Tomate, die nicht mit irgendeinem Konservierungsmittel eingeschmiert war.

Aus: *Ein Sowjet-Journalist über den amerikanischen Lebensstil*, in: *Der Spiegel* 15/1967.

Commentary

1 **whether** — sei es: or *whether it be*. Students frequently produced *be it,* which is grammatically possible, but has rather antiquated connotations, and thus is inappropriate in this modern American context.
1 **during a meal** — beim Essen: also possible *over, at*. However *over* in *over a cup of coffee* cannot be replaced by another preposition.
1 **dinner** — Bankett: whereas *dinner* in this context refers to a formal occasion, *banquet* would refer to a particularly sumptuous type of dinner. SOED

10. A Soviet Journalist on the American Way of Life (2)

Whether during a meal, over a cup of coffee or at a dinner, there are three topics of conversation Americans can never avoid — their cars, their digestion and their insomnia.

Americans don't lay out gardens in front of their houses. They sow a thick
5 lawn, which they mow once a week and water six times a week. In America houses only rarely have a fence. Only very expensive villas, old parks, jails and madhouses are surrounded by high fences with strong iron gates ...

Americans think extremely practically and economically. While the husband is attempting to get a rise at the office, his wife is permanently
10 concerned with reducing the house-keeping costs. The wives scan the newspapers frequently to find out what goods are being sold particularly cheaply so that they can boast in the evening at supper of having saved half-a-dollar on a pair of shoes, 25 cents on a shirt, 40 cents on four bottles of Italian olive oil and 60 cents on two pounds of meat. All the time and
15 wherever they are, Americans drink enormous quantities of coffee. If they can't pep themselves up with it, they soon become surly and irritable, and can't work anymore.

During the three years I lived in New York, I was never sold a rotten egg, a wormy apple or rancid butter. But I never ate a tasty fresh egg either, or a
20 cucumber or a tomato that hadn't been smeared with some kind of preserving agent.

(p. 144,1) describes it as "now usu. a ceremonial or state feast, followed by speeches". As only relatively few Americans would ever be present on such an occasion *dinner* seems the preferable translation.
1 **there are three topics** — drei Gesprächsthemen: the German text places the stress on the object of the sentence, *drei Gesprächsthemen,* by inverting the word order. The same effect can be achieved in English by singling out *topics (there are three topics),* thus placing the focus of the sentence on it,

and giving the rest of the information in a relative clause. The version *the Americans can never avoid three topics of conversation*, while being grammatically correct, does not convey the relative stress of the German.

3 **insomnia** – Schlaflosigkeit: also *sleeplessness*.
4 **lay out** – legen ... an: it is possible to *plant flowers*, or *plant a garden with flowers*, but *plant a garden* in the sense of 'create a garden' sounds rather odd.
5 **water** – sprengen: also *sprinkle*.
6 **have a fence** – werden umzäunt: also *are fenced round* or *fences are only rarely erected around houses*.
6 **expensive villas** – teure Villen: possibly *mansions*, which would refer to large, probably older, stately houses. *Luxury home* would be more appropriate to a house-agent's advert or catalogue.
6 **jails and madhouses** – Gefängnisse und Irrenanstalten: the translation here is affected by a question of style. The author is deliberately seeking to shock the reader by the juxtaposition of very disparate things (*villas, parks/jails, madhouses*). Thus *madhouse*, or *lunatic asylum*, both of which would normally be avoided in enlightened circles because of their pejorative connotations in favour of the neutral *mental hospital*, are more appropriate in this context than *mental hospital*, which would not achieve the effect intended.
8 **practically and economically** – praktisch und wirtschaftlich: possible variant: *(think) in practical and economic(al) terms*. Many students failed to recognize the adverbial function of *praktisch* and *wirtschaftlich* and translated them wrongly as **(think) practical and economic*.

The choice between *economic* and *economical* is usually quite clear, *economic* having reference to economy in the sense of the financial state, for example, of a country (*the economy of Great Britain, the economic system of Great Britain*), and *economical* to economy in the sense of a means of spending less money (*one of her economies was to buy margarine instead of butter, eating margarine is more economical than eating butter*). In this text, however, *wirtschaftlich* expresses both 'in terms of household economy' and 'in terms of spending less money'. Thus in this case, if an adjective is used in the translation, either *economic* or *economical* would be possible, the preference being given to *economic* as it covers a wider range of meanings than *economical*.

9 **husband** – Mann: also possible here *man*.
9 **rise** – Gehaltserhöhungen: also *increase in salary*. Note that salaries are usually paid monthly, and are calculated on an annual income, whereas

wages are usually paid weekly and calculated on an hourly rate. *Salary* is more likely in this text.
9 **is permanently concerned with** — ist ... ständig bemüht: variants: *permanently looking out for ways of, permanently on the look-out for ways of.*
10 **reducing** — senken: variants: *lowering, cutting, cutting down.*
10 **house-keeping costs** — Haushaltungskosten: *living-costs* would be very unusual. *Cost of living* is inappropriate here, as this implies the average cost involved in clothing, feeding, housing, etc. a family of a given size, in a given country or area, at a given time. To reduce the cost of living would involve exerting influence on manufacturers to reduce their prices.
10 **scan** — durchblättern: *skim* might be possible here, though we have avoided this as being inappropriate since it seems to suggest a certain superficiality and lack of intention in reading, whereas the American wives, according to the text, presumably have a very clear intention of what they are looking for and will read the special offers they find with great care.
12 **boast** — sich ... rühmen: note the *of -ing* construction after *boast*. **Boast to have saved* is unacceptable.
12 **saved** — gespart: not *spared* (interference from *sparen*!).
13 **on a pair of shoes** — bei einem Paar Schuhe: *on* is the only possible preposition here.
14 **all the time and wherever they are** — immer und überall: this is difficult to translate satisfactorily. The force of *immer und überall* lies in the juxtaposition of the two elements, and in the balance, or symmetry, of the two single-word adverbs. The combination *always and everywhere* sounds odd, probably because *always* would most naturally occur before the verb (*Americans always drink* ...), *everywhere* on the other hand at the end of the sentence (*Americans always drink coffee everywhere*). Here the juxtaposition is lost, and as *everywhere* would be better replaced by *wherever they are*, the balance is lost, too. A possible version which renders juxtaposition and balance is *at any time, at any place*. The version which probably best renders the stress on both items is *Americans are always drinking coffee, no matter where they are*, whereby the use of the Present Progressive with *always* renders a degree of irritation at this coffee-drinking habit on the part of the speaker, thus strengthening the force of *always* to provide a balanced counterpart to *no matter where they are.*
15 **enormous quantities** — Unmengen: *huge, large, vast,* and *tremendous* also collocate with *quantities.*
15 **if they can't pep themselves up with it** — wenn sie sich nicht damit aufputschen können: variants: *if they can't stimulate themselves with it, if*

they haven't got it to stimulate themselves with/as a stimulant/as a pick-me-up.
16 **soon** – schnell: also *quickly, in no time.*
16 **surly** – mürrisch: also *bad-tempered, ill-tempered, cross, irascible.*
17 **can't work anymore** – können nicht mehr arbeiten: also *are no longer able to work.*
18 **I was never sold** – hat man mir kein einziges Mal ... verkauft: also *no one ever sold me. Sell* is what Quirk et al. call a ditransitive verb (see p. 843). In this example the indirect object of the active sentence *no one ever sold me a rotten egg* becomes the subject in the passive transformation (*I was sold* ...). The direct object *a rotten egg* could also become subject of a passive sentence *a rotten egg was sold to me by no one/a rotten egg was never sold to me by anyone.* Not **one never sold me. One* implies people in general,

11. Fragen der Sozialpolitik

Großbritannien, das als erstes europäisches Land den Wohlfahrtsstaat verwirklicht hat, bekam auch alle Nachteile zu spüren, weil die wachsenden Leistungen auf sozialen Gebieten und die Konkurrenz mit anderen Industriestaaten zwar hohe Anforderungen an Arbeitszeit und Leistung stellen, beides aber verringert wurde. Die Konsequenz ist für jeden offensichtlich. Die Wettbewerbsfähigkeit der britischen Industrie ist wesentlich geringer, als sie sein könnte. Großbritannien könnte bei seinem hohen Standard industrieller Fähigkeiten und Wissens mit Leichtigkeit seinen Rang in der Industriewelt zurückgewinnen, würden die Arbeitszeit und die Arbeitsintensität zu früheren Normen zurückgeführt.

In Frankreich sind die Verhältnisse nicht so extrem. Aber die ständige Abwertung des französischen Franken ist auch ein wichtiges Indiz dafür, daß man nicht hohe Leistungen erwarten kann, wenn nicht auch die dafür erforderliche Arbeitszeit und -intensität angeboten werden.

Die Beispiele lassen sich vermehren. Man könnte auch noch Schweden nennen, das mit seinem hohen sozialen Standard, trotz seiner Nichtbeteiligung an zwei Weltkriegen, trotz der hohen Gewinne, die es aus beiden Weltkriegen gezogen hat, heute hinsichtlich seiner industriellen Wettbewerbsfähigkeit nicht mehr sehr hoch bewertet wird.

In der bundesdeutschen Diskussion und Wirklichkeit werden heute zwei Auswege angeboten beziehungsweise praktiziert: 1. die Beschäftigung von ausländischen Arbeitnehmern und 2. Steuererhöhungen, umschrieben als

including the speaker. *One* in *one should never sell rotten fruit* implies 'everybody, including you and me ...'
18 **a rotten egg** — ein verfaultes Ei: also *a bad egg*, not **a foul egg*, *foul* not being used in collocation with *egg* in the meaning *verfault*.
19 **a wormy apple** — einen wurmstichigen Apfel: also *an apple with a worm in it*, or *a maggoty apple*. Not *a worm-eaten apple*. *Worm-eaten* is most commonly used in connection with furniture attacked by wood-worm.
19 **I ... ate** — ich habe ... gegessen: Simple Past tense because the period referred to is clearly completed and has no reference to the present to justify the use of the Present Perfect tense.
20 **cucumber** — Gurke: or *gherkin*. It is not clear from the text which kind of *Gurke* is meant.
20 **smeared** — eingeschmiert: *treated* is also possible, though it doesn't have the negative connotations of *einschmieren* and *smear*.

---

11. Questions of Social Policy

Great Britain, which was the first European country to set up the welfare state, also felt all its disadvantages, because while increased benefits in the social sphere and competition with other industrial nations place high demands on working-hours and output, both of these were in fact reduced.
5 The result is obvious to everyone. British industry is considerably less competitive than it could be. With its high standard of industrial skills and know-how Great Britain could easily recover its position in the industrial world, if working-hours and productivity were brought back to earlier norms.

In France conditions are not so extreme. But the continual devaluation of
10 the French franc is also an important indication of the fact that you cannot expect a high level of production unless the necessary working-hours and productivity are also offered.

There are many other examples. One could also take Sweden, which, with its high social standard, is not rated very highly these days as far as its
15 industrial competitiveness is concerned, despite the fact that it did not participate in two world wars and despite the high profits it made out of both.

Today in West Germany, in debate and in practice, two solutions are being proposed or actually put into operation: 1. the employment of foreign
20 workers and 2. tax increases, euphemistically described as a reduction in consumption in favour of public spending. But these solutions are illusory.

Konsumverzicht zugunsten öffentlicher Leistungen. Das aber sind nur Scheinlösungen.

Die Beschäftigung von weit über zwei, in naher Zukunft vielleicht drei und mehr Millionen ausländischer Arbeitnehmer bringt eine Unzahl von schwerwiegenden Problemen mit sich, die in kurzer Zeit ähnlich schwer auf uns lasten werden wie in den Vereinigten Staaten das Rassenproblem auf der Gesellschaft lastet.

Aus: H. H. Karry, *Abschied von einer Illusion,* in: *Die Zeit* 39/1972.

Commentary

Questions of Social Policy – Fragen der Sozialpolitik: also ... *concerning social policy.* Not *politics*, which is concerned with the science or art of government, whereas *policy* refers to a plan or course of action in a certain field.

Both the English *question* and the German *Frage* can have the meaning of 'something which is asked' and also a meaning approximating to 'problem'. Here we have the meaning 'problem'. The prepositions *of* and *concerning* collocate with *question* in this meaning, whereas *on* or *about* collocate with *question* meaning 'something which is asked'. Thus *questions on social policy* and *questions about social policy* are both inappropriate here.

1 **Great Britain, which was** – Großbritannien, das: a non-defining relative clause, therefore preceded by a comma. Students found this very difficult to understand. As *Great Britain* is unique it can only in very special circumstances be followed by a defining relative clause, i.e. be defined in such a way as to distinguish it from another Great Britain, e.g. *The Great Britain of today is very different from the Great Britain I used to know before the war.* Alternative constructions: *Great Britain, the first country to/that.* The construction *being the first country to ..., Great Britain ...,* while grammatically correct, implies a causality ('since Great Britain was the first country ...') not suggested by the German text, and is thus inappropriate.

1 **the first ... country to** – als erstes ... Land: also *the first country that. The first country which,* although not absolutely wrong, would be unlikely, *first* in this context normally collocating with *to* + infinitive or *that* + relative clause. A translation such as *Great Britain, which as the first ... country* is unacceptable.

1 **set up** – verwirklicht: also *put into practice, make ... reality,* possibly *put into effect, introduce. Realize* is unlikely here.

The employment of far more than two million, and in the near future possibly three and more million foreign workers involves a host of serious problems which will soon weigh just as heavy on us as the racial problem does
25 on American society.

1 **the welfare state** — den Wohlfahrtsstaat: the omission of the determiner is a frequent mistake. *Welfare state,* though abstract, is countable, and as such requires a determiner, here either *the* or *a,* depending on the point of view of the speaker. Seen as a specific concept — and at the time of its founding it was unique — it would take *the;* seen from the point of view of the present, when other welfare states exist, it would take the indefinite *a.*
2 **felt** — bekam zu spüren: also *experienced, suffered, was faced with, was confronted with, was made to feel,* possibly *had to experience, had to suffer.*
2 **all its disadvantages** — alle Nachteile: the zero article (*all disadvantages*) would be used for generic reference, whereas here the reference is to specific disadvantages, and therefore either the definite article or *its* must be used (see Quirk et al., p. 153).
2 **while** —: also *whereas, although.* The relationship between the two clauses depending on *because* can be made clearer if one of the above conjunctions is used with the first clause.
2 **benefits** — Leistungen: also *services.* Not *performances* or *achievements.*
2 **in the social sphere** — auf sozialen Gebieten: note that the singular form would be more likely in English. Variants for *sphere: sector, field.*
3 **industrial nations** — Industriestaaten: also *industrialized nations.* Possibly ... *countries; states,* though not wrong, would be less likely.
3 **place high demands on** — hohe Anforderungen an ... stellen: also *make high/great demands on.*
4 **output** — Leistung: also *production, productivity.*
4 **reduced** — verringert: variants: *cut (back),* possibly *decreased, diminished;* not *curtailed,* which would imply that working-hours and output had been deliberately reduced, possibly as they were considered to be too large.

69

5 **result** – Konsequenz: note that *consequences*, which can be used here as a variant for *result*, usually occurs in the plural form if it is not in a set phrase such as *in consequence of* (= 'as a result of'), *of no consequence* (= 'of no importance').

5 **British industry is ... competitive** – die Wettbewerbsfähigkeit der britischen Industrie : also *the competitiveness of British industry*. Note that while *concurrence* does exist in English, the meanings of *Konkurrenz* and *concurrence* are totally different, the latter implying either 'agreement' or 'the fact of two things happening at the same time'.

A common mistake was the use of the definite article with *British industry*, which in this context is a mass noun and takes the zero determiner. *The British industries* (countable) implies several specific branches such as the textile industry, the petro-chemical industry, etc.

5 **considerably** – wesentlich: also *substantially*, not *essentially*.

6 **could** – könnte: also *might*. Both *could* and *might* here express possibility.

6 **with its high standard** – bei seinem hohen Standard: *high* could be omitted, as *standard* in this context implies 'high standard'. The possessive pronoun *her* instead of *its* can be used to refer to Great Britain, and later to Sweden, but if it is used it must be used consistently throughout the text.

6 **skills** – Fähigkeiten: also *expertise*.

7 **know-how** – Wissens: *knowledge* would probably be avoided in this context in favour of *know-how*, which implies not just 'knowledge' but 'the knowledge of how to do something, based on experience'.

7 **could** – könnte: here *could* expresses hypothetical ability, in other words both the elements of possibility and ability, ('because Great Britain has the ability ..., it would be possible for her ...'). While *might* is possible here, it is less likely than *could* as it merely expresses the possibility, and not the ability.

7 **recover** – zurückgewinnen: also *win back, regain*, not *gain back*.

7 **position** – Rang: also *status, standing*.

8 **productivity** – Arbeitsintensität: also *the relationship between manpower and production*. *Working-intensity, intensity of work* might just be possible.

8 **brought back** – zurückgeführt: also *restored, readjusted*. Other variants: *if earlier norms for working-hours ... were reinforced/reintroduced, if working-hours ... reverted to earlier norms*. *Led back* is not possible here, as it would refer to the spatial dimension.

8 **norms** – Normen: also *standards*.

9 **continual** —ständige: also *continuous, steady, constant, perpetual*. *Permanent* seems an unlikely choice here as this refers more to an unchangeable state than a process which could be reversed.
10 **is an important indication** — ist ... ein wichtiges Indiz: also *provides us with significant evidence*. Not *proof*, as this goes a stage further than *Indiz*, *indication*, and *evidence*.
11 **a high level of production** — hohe Leistungen: students were divided on their interpretation of *Leistungen*, some considering it to refer to 'soziale Leistungen' (*a wide range of social services*), others to 'Leistungen im industriellen Bereich' (*a high level of production*).
13 **there are many other examples** — die Beispiele lassen sich vermehren: also *many other examples/plenty of other examples could be given/mentioned*. Not *the examples can be multiplied*, which is unidiomatic.
13 **take** — nennen: also *cite, quote, refer to*.
14 **rated** — bewertet: not *estimated*, which means 'approximately calculated'. Not *valuated*, which is not listed in SOED.
14 **not ... these days** — heute ... nicht mehr: also *no longer*.
14 **as far as its industrial competitiveness is concerned** — hinsichtlich seiner industriellen Wettbewerbsfähigkeit: variants: *from the point of view of/as regards its industrial competitiveness, as an industrially competitive country, as regards its ability to compete industrially*. Note that **its ability of competing* is grammatically unacceptable.
15 **despite** — trotz: note the constructions *despite* + N, *in spite of* + N.
15 **despite the fact that it did not participate** — trotz seiner Nichtbeteiligung: also *although it did not participate/take part, although it was not involved, despite its non-participation/non-involvement*, or, simply, *despite its neutrality*.
16 **profits** — Gewinne: also *gains*. Not *winnings*, which is usually applied to the money won in gambling or betting.
16 **it made out of** — die es aus ... gezogen hat: also *it drew from/out of, which accrued to it from*.
18 **in West Germany, in debate and in practice** — in der bundesdeutschen Diskussion und Wirklichkeit: the most common translation ran something like *in West Germany's discussion and reality*, which is not very satisfactory, partly as it is too vague, partly as other words would be used in this context. Note that *the Federal Republic* or *Federal Germany* can also be used.
18 **are being proposed** — werden angeboten: although the use of the Present Simple could also be justified, the Present Progressive seems more likely

71

here, as it stresses that the solutions are not solutions for all time, but the solutions which are at the moment under consideration. This is implied in the German text by the inclusion of *heute* indicating a limited period, and *Scheinlösungen*, indicating that these solutions will not be valid for long.
19 **proposed** — angeboten: also *suggested, put forward.*
19 **or actually put into operation** — beziehungsweise praktiziert: as usual, the translation of *beziehungsweise* proved problematical. *Respectively* might just about be possible after *put into operation*, but is impossible preceding it. It is probably best to avoid it here completely, and use *or* instead.
Students were divided on their interpretation of the importance of *beziehungsweise*. To some it meant little more than 'or', to others, however, it stressed the duality (*Diskussion, angeboten/Wirklichkeit, praktiziert*) more than *or*. For this reason we added *actually* to *put into operation*, in order to stress the difference. Another possibility is *or rather*. Variants for *put into operation: carried out,* or *put into practice, practised,* if *practice* has not been used for *Wirklichkeit*. Note the spelling of *practice* (noun) and *to practise.*
20 **workers** — Arbeitnehmern: also the mass noun *labour*. Not *employees*, if *employment* has been used (*the employment of employees*), as the workers can only become employees after they have been employed, and as the phrase would be avoided for stylistic reasons. Not labourers, which is usually applied to workers who do the particularly heavy, manual, unskilled work in various trades, e.g. *a builder's labourer*. *Labourer* corresponds to a certain extent to the German *Hilfsarbeiter.*
20 **euphemistically described** — umschrieben: this translation is based on an interpretation of *umschrieben* as a deliberate attempt to make the tax-increases more acceptable to the public. This is of course not the only interpretation, and the translations *circumscribed, paraphrased, characterized* are all less extreme in their interpretation.

---

12. Texte im Anfangsunterricht

Was sind die Gründe für das häufige Vorkommen des sogenannten Mess-muddle-and-confusion-Erzählgerüsts in den Texten der Anfangslektionen im Fremdsprachenunterricht?
Da ist zunächst einmal der *jugendpsychologische Aspekt* zu bedenken. Daß das „Unordnungs-Schema" die Schüler in diesem Alter anspricht, weiß wohl jeder Lehrer aus Erfahrung: je toller das Durcheinander, um so mehr sind die Kinder dabei. Spielt der Lehrbuchverfasser hier mit, vermag er zwei Fliegen

20 **reduction in consumption** — Konsumverzicht: also possible *restricted consumption, restraint in consumption,* possibly *cut-back in consumers' demands, sacrifices on the part of the consumer.*
21 **public spending** — öffentlicher Leistungen: *Leistungen* is rather vague, and so we have a series of possible translations, depending on the interpretation: *public services, public benefits, public expenditure.*
21 **but these solutions are illusory** — das sind aber nur Scheinlösungen: also *these are only apparent solutions, these only seem/appear to be solutions, these only seem to solve the problem, these are only pseudo-solutions.*
22 **two million foreign workers** — zwei ... Millionen ausländischer Arbeitnehmer: note the frequent mistake **two millions of foreign workers.* When *million* is used in an actual number and precedes a noun, then it is not marked for plural, and it is not followed by *of,* for example, *two million workers, three dozen eggs, five thousand pounds.* When *million, dozen, thousand,* etc. are used to express not a specific number, but a general large amount, then they are marked for plural and followed by *of,* for example, *there were thousands of birds sitting on the telegraph wires, we wrote dozens of essays at school.*
23 **involves** — bringt ... mit sich: also *entails, causes, brings with it.*
23 **host** — Unzahl: also *multitude, enormous/vast/huge quantity/number. Series, number, quantity* without a modifier such as *vast* or *enormous* do not imply the great size suggested in *Unzahl.*
23 **serious** — schwerwiegenden: also *grave,* possibly *far-reaching.*
24 **heavy** — schwer: also *heavily.* Note that after *weigh, lay, sit,* usually in a figurative sense, the adjective form *heavy* can replace the adverb form *heavily,* for example, *his unfulfilled promise lay heavy on his mind.*

12. Texts in Lessons for Beginners

What are the reasons behind the frequent occurrence of the so-called mess-muddle-and-confusion narrative structure in the texts in the initial stages of foreign language teaching?

First of all there is the aspect of child psychology to be taken into
5 consideration. The "confusion pattern" appeals to children of this age, as every teacher well knows from experience: the wilder the muddle, the more the children are involved. If the text-book author plays along, he can kill two

mit einem Schlag zu treffen: er kann die spröden Sach- und Stoffbereiche der unmittelbaren Umwelt der Kinder eingliedern, und er kann dies – eben mittels des M-M-C-Erzählgerüsts – auf eine Weise tun, die ihm die innere Beteiligung der Kinder sichert. Der jugendpsychologische Aspekt hat also auch Konsequenzen für das anzubietende Sprachmaterial.

Zum andern müssen wir den *lerntheoretischen Aspekt* betrachten. Es ist keinesfalls so, daß nur bestimmte und allein für den Anfangsunterricht typische Sprachelemente zur Ausformung des M-M-C-Erzählgerüsts in Frage kommen; eine Vielfalt von grammatischen und lexikalischen *teaching items* ist darin offensichtlich einzuarbeiten. Nicht *was* in diesem Erzählgerüst sprachlich unterzubringen ist, sondern *wie* es darin unterzubringen ist, das macht, so glauben wir, seine besondere Eignung für den Anfangsunterricht aus. Das lerntheoretische und unterrichtsmethodische Geheimnis liegt offenbar in dem additiven Aufbau dieses Erzählgerüsts. Sein ausgeprägter Zug zur Reihung, zur Wiederholung von sprachlich Gleichem oder Ähnlichem, macht das M-M-C-Gerüst für den Fremdsprachenunterricht so interessant. Texte, die nach dem M-M-C-Schema verfaßt und geschickt angelegt sind, können sich als verkappte *Substitution Tables* entpuppen, als *Substitution Tables*, deren großer Vorzug die Einbeziehung der zu übenden grammatischen und lexikalischen Elemente in eine Situation ist – im Gegensatz zu den rein formalen *Pattern-Drill-Tables* älterer, Palmerscher Prägung. Die gleichzeitige Struktur- und Situationsbewußtheit, wie sie neuere linguistische und lerntheoretische Erkenntnisse fordern, findet somit im M-M-C-Erzählgerüst ihren textgestalterischen Niederschlag.

Aus: H.-J. Lechler, *Lust und Unlust im Englischunterricht.* Stuttgart: Ernst Klett, 1972.

Commentary

in Lessons for Beginners – im Anfangsunterricht: also *in classes for beginners, in the first lessons, in elementary instruction, in the elementary stages.* Possible is *for the teaching of beginners,* but not *for beginners' teaching,* which would imply that the beginners were teaching rather than being taught. Not *for primary teaching,* as *primary* refers to education between the ages of five and eleven, in primary or junior schools.

1 **what** – was: *which* is inappropriate here, as it would refer to some already existing number of reasons from which a selection was to be made, whereas *what* seeks a definition of the reasons.

birds with one stone: he can integrate the dull subject matter into the children's immediate environment, and he can do so — by means of this very M-M-C narrative structure — in such a way as to ensure the children's inner participation. Thus the child psychology aspect has consequences for the language material to be offered.

Secondly, we must consider the aspect of learning theory. It is definitely not the case that only certain language elements, namely those typical of the elementary stages of language learning, are suitable for the filling-out of the M-M-C narrative structure; a great number of grammatical and lexical teaching items can obviously be integrated into it. It is not *what* can be accommodated in this narrative framework in the way of language, but *how* it can be accommodated that in our opinion makes it particularly suitable for the elementary stages of teaching. The secret from the point of view of learning theory and teaching methodology clearly lies in the additive structure of this narrative framework. Its distinct tendency to catenation, to the repetition of the same or similar language elements, makes it of such interest to foreign language teaching. Texts composed according to the M-M-C pattern and skilfully presented can turn out to be substitution tables in disguise, substitution tables whose major advantage is that they include the grammatical and lexical items to be practised in a situation, in contrast to the strictly formal pattern-drill tables of the older Palmer sort. Thus the simultaneous perception of structure and situation, as demanded by recent findings in linguistics and learning theory, finds its textual realization in the M-M-C narrative pattern.

1 **behind** — für: also *for.*
1 **the frequent occurrence** — das häufige Vorkommen: also *the fact that ... occurs/appears so frequently.*
2 **narrative structure** — Erzählgerüsts: also *narrative pattern, framework.*
4 **first of all** — zunächst einmal: also *to begin with, to start with, for a start.*
4 **there is ... to be taken into consideration** — da ist ... zu bedenken: also *to be considered, to be taken into account.* This structure places the emphasis on the child psychology aspect, as the German text does. Alternative structures such as ... *must be taken into consideration, we must take*

account of..., *account must be taken of...*, do not place the emphasis so clearly.
4 **the aspect of child psychology** — der jugendpsychologische Aspekt: *youth psychology* would be rather unusual. **Child psychological aspect* is unacceptable.
5 **the "confusion pattern" appeals** — daß das „Unordnungs-Schema" ... anspricht: again a question of emphasis. The subordinate *daß*-clause is emphasized in the German by being placed at the beginning of the sentence. To translate the sentence as *every teacher knows that...*, while grammatically correct, does not convey the emphasis in the German; hence our translation, which retains the stress-pattern by changing the main clause to a subordinate clause and vice versa, thus keeping *the confusion pattern* at the beginning.
6 **every teacher** — jeder Lehrer: the reference is to a large unspecified group, and the emphasis on the component of meaning 'all teachers' rather than 'the individual teacher', therefore *each teacher* is inappropriate here.
6 **the wilder the muddle** — je toller das Durcheinander: here there are many possible translations, for example, *the madder/crazier/merrier the muddle/confusion/disorder*.
6 **the more the children are involved** — um so mehr sind die Kinder dabei: variants: *the greater the children's involvement, the more they pay attention, the more their attention is held*. Note that *engaged/engagement* cannot replace *involved/involvement* here. Versions such as *the greater their engagement, the more they are engaged* are examples of interference resulting from the German *engagiert* as a near-synonym for *sind dabei*.
7 **plays along** — spielt ... mit: also *plays along with this, joins in this game, bears this in mind, makes use of this*.
7 **kill two birds with one stone** — zwei Fliegen mit einem Schlag zu treffen: it is advisable either to translate a proverb with a proverb, if there is an appropriate one, or to interpret its meaning, but not to translate it literally or even to invent a new proverb. Here a possible interpretative rendering might be *achieve two things at one stroke*.
8 **the dull subject matter** — die spröden Sach- und Stoffbereiche: *subject matter* is sufficiently wide in scope to cover *Sach- und Stoffbereiche*. *Dry* is a possible variant for *dull*. Here we have a problem of interpretation. Students were almost equally divided on their interpretation of the relationship between *Sach- und Stoffbereiche* and *Umwelt*. Some perceived the relationship to be as in *er kann die spröden Stoffbereiche in die Welt der Kinder eingliedern;* to others it was as in *er kann die der*

Kinderwelt angehörenden spröden Stoffbereiche in seine Texte eingliedern. The difference is reflected in the choice between the prepositions *of* or *in*, the choice reflecting a radical difference in interpretation.
9 **by means of this very M-M-C ...** — eben mittels des M-M-C ...: *eben* modifies *M-M-C* rather than *mittels*, thus *this very M-M-C*, and not *by the very means*.
10 **in such a way as to** — auf eine Weise, die: alternative, though rather less idiomatic, structure: *in such a way that (he can ensure ...).* Note that whereas *that* here introduces a resultative clause, *that* in the structure *in a way that (ensures him)* is a relative pronoun introducing a relative clause, and is the subject of that relative clause. Thus versions such as **in a way that he ensures ...* are unacceptable.
11 **has consequences for** — hat ... Konsequenzen für: also *affects, has a direct bearing on, has implications for, is of consequence for.*
12 **the language material to be offered** — das anzubietende Sprachmaterial: also *the choice/selection of language material.*
13 **secondly** — zum andern: this refers back to *zunächst einmal* at the beginning of the first paragraph. Also possible *on the other hand, moreover, in addition.*
13 **the aspect of learning theory** — den lerntheoretischen Aspekt: variant: *the theory of learning aspect.* The theoretical aspect of learning is not quite the same thing, as this suggests an opposition to *the practical aspect of learning* whereas the opposition is to *the aspect of child psychology.*
13 **it is definitely not the case** — es ist keinesfalls so: also *it is certainly not true, it is certainly wrong.* Negative adverbs placed initially are followed by inversion, thus if *by no means* is used initially, then the following subject and verb must be inverted.
15 **are suitable for** — in Frage kommen: variants: *come into consideration, can be considered, can be used,* but not *can be called into question,* which means 'can be doubted'.
15 **filling-out** — Ausformung: *forming* and *formation* are not really appropriate, as it is not a case of forming the structure, but of adding to the structure in order to make the complete narrative.
16 **a great number** — eine Vielfalt: also *a great variety, an abundance, a multitude, a wide spectrum.*
17 **obviously** — offensichtlich: also *evidently, clearly.* Also *it is evident/obvious/ clear/apparent that,* but not *apparently.* While *apparent* implies 'easy/clear to see', *apparently* implies 'it seems that'.
17 **can be integrated** — ist einzuarbeiten: also *included, fitted in.* Again we have a

case of varying interpretations here. The opposition in the two parts of the sentence 'it is not true that only a few elements can be fitted into the M-M-C pattern – on the contrary, many elements can be fitted in' seems to suggest a translation with *can*, but many students felt that *ist einzuarbeiten* meant 'soll eingearbeitet werden', and accordingly translated it as *must be integrated*. The English structure *are to be integrated* is, like the German, ambiguous, and is probably the best way out of the dilemma.

18 **in the way of language** – sprachlich: also *(what can be accommodated) in the way of language elements/linguistically/from the language point of view/from the linguistic point of view,* although versions including *linguistic/linguistically* are probably best avoided here since they refer strictly speaking to the science of language, rather than language.

19 **makes it particularly suitable** – macht ... seine besondere Eignung ... aus: also *constitutes its particular/special suitability/value/appropriateness.*

20 **the secret from the point of view of learning theory and teaching methodology** – das lerntheoretische und unterrichtsmethodische Geheimnis: as English does not possess adjectives equivalent to *lerntheoretisch* and *unterrichtsmethodisch,* these need to be expressed nominally, whereby the question of the relationship between them and *Geheimnis* is important for the choice of preposition. *The secret of learning theory* implies 'learning theory has a secret', whereas the German text implies 'the narrative framework has a secret, which regarded from the point of view of learning theory ... can be seen to lie in the additive structure'. Hence *the secret of learning theory* is wrong here as it does not translate the meaning expressed in the German text. The adjective forms in **the learning-theoretical and teaching-method(olog)ical secret* are unacceptable; an example of interference, they reflect a form of adjective-building in German which is not paralleled in English.

21 **additive** – additiven: not *additional*. In this context *additive* corresponds closely in meaning to the active Present Participle 'adding', and *additional* to the passive Past Participle 'added'. Thus *an additive structure* expresses a meaning approximating to 'a structure which adds' and *an additional structure* a meaning approximating to 'a structure which is added', 'an extra structure'.

21 **structure** – Aufbau: also *construction, build-up.*

22 **its distinct tendency** – sein ausgeprägter Zug: also *marked/strong tendency.*

22 **catenation** – Reihung: *catenation* is the usual technical term here. *Sequence* might also be possible.

23 **of the same or similar language elements** – von sprachlich Gleichem oder

Ähnlichem: also *of what is linguistically the same or similar*. *Identical* is a possible variant for *the same*, but not *equivalent*, which implies 'of the same value but not identical'.
23 **of such interest** – so interessant: also *so interesting*, possibly *so relevant*.
24 **composed** – verfaßt: also *written*, possibly *constructed*.
25 **skilfully presented** – geschickt angelegt: also *skilfully/cleverly arranged/ organized/planned*.
25 **turn out to be** – sich ... entpuppen: also *reveal themselves to be*.
25 **substitution tables in disguise** – verkappte Substitution Tables: also *disguised/camouflaged/hidden substitution tables*.
26 **whose major advantage** – deren großer Vorzug: also *the major advantage of which*. *Whose* does not have a solely personal reference, but can also be used in place of *of which*. Both *great* and *greatest* are possible as variants for *major*.
27 **to be practised** – zu übenden: also possibly *to be learnt*. Not *to be exercised*. *To exercise* can be used roughly in the meaning of 'to give practice to', 'to give movement to' in contexts such as *to exercise a horse, to exercise a stiff wrist*.
28 **strictly formal** – rein formalen: also *purely formal*, but not *merely formal*, as this suggests 'only formal', and thus that the M-M-C texts are formal, too, but with the addition of some other characteristic, which is not the case.
29 **perception** – -bewußtheit: also *apprehension*, possibly *awareness*. *Consciousness* is unlikely here, as it seems too stative in its meaning to be compatible with *simultaneous*.
29 **as demanded by** – wie sie ... fordern: also *required by;* not *requested by*, which is too weak.
29 **recent** – neuere: not *modern*. The distinction between *modern* and *recent* in this context can be explained as follows: *recent* refers to a period of time near to present time, yet clearly in the past, whereas *modern* refers to a period of time around the present, i. e. including the near past (the recent past), the present, and continuing into the future. The findings referred to in the text were clearly made in the past. This makes the collocation *modern findings* unlikely here. It would be possible to say *the findings of modern linguistics and learning theory*, since modern linguistics and learning theory are not bound to actual time as for example the publication of findings is, but this is not an exact translation of *neuere linguistische und lerntheoretische Erkenntnisse*.
30 **its textual realization** – ihren textgestalterischen Niederschlag: or more precisely *the means for its textual realization*. Also *its creative expression*.

13. Über die 20er Jahre

Die Frage, wann Vergangenheit beginnt Geschichte zu werden, wird von einigen Büchern über die Weimarer Republik und ihr kulturelles Erbe angeschnitten, die kürzlich in Amerika erschienen sind. Für diejenigen, die sie überlebten, ist die Weimarer Republik ein Stück Vergangenheit, das in die Gegenwart hineinragt. Für die Jugend und das Ausland aber ist sie, mehr oder weniger, eine abgeschlossene historische Epoche, ein Mythos, dessen Wirklichkeitsgehalt durch Stichworte wie Bauhaus, zwanziger Jahre, Dreigroschenoper, Marlene Dietrich, erschöpft zu sein scheint.

In Amerika ist dieser Mythos in letzter Zeit mehrfach Gegenstand umfangreicher akademischer Untersuchungen geworden. Man beginnt, sich bewußt zu werden, wie sehr die Republik von Weimar dazu beigetragen hat, das Gesicht dieses Jahrhunderts zu prägen, vor allem in Amerika, wo so viele ihrer bedeutendsten Repräsentanten nach dem Zusammenbruch Zuflucht fanden. Laura Fermi, die Witwe des Atomphysikers und Nobelpreisträgers Enrico Fermi, gibt in ihrem grundlegenden Werk „Berühmte Emigranten" einen Begriff von den Ausmaßen und der Tragweite jener Abwanderung des Geistes aus Europa.

Einen weiteren Beitrag zu diesem Thema leistet der von der „Harvard University Press" herausgegebene Sammelband „The Intellectual Migration". Autoren wie Paul Lazarsfeld, T. W. Adorno und der Atomphysiker Leo Szilard schreiben darin über die Bedeutung exilierter Wissenschaftler für die Entstehung eines modernen Bewußtseins in Amerika. In diesem Zusammenhang muß auch der bedeutende Band über das Bauhaus von Hans M. Wingler erwähnt werden, der soeben vom „Massachusetts Institute of Technology" in englischer Sprache herausgebracht wurde. Es ist vielleicht kein Zufall, daß das Erscheinungsjahr 1969 der amerikanischen Ausgabe zugleich das Todesjahr der beiden Großen des Bauhauses, Walter Gropius und Mies van der Rohe, ist.

Aus: Hans Sahl, *Über die 20er Jahre,* in: *Die Welt* 6. 11. 1969.

Commentary

1 **the question as to when** – die Frage, wann: also *the question of when.* The question *when* seems unusual.
1 **begins to become** – beginnt ... zu werden: also *starts to be/become.*
1 **touched on** – angeschnitten: the German text suggests that the subject was not dealt with fully. Acceptable variants would be *mentioned,* and also

13. On the Twenties

The question as to when the past begins to become history is touched on in several books on the Weimar Republic and its cultural heritage which were recently published in America. For those who survived it, the Weimar Republic is a piece of history that reaches down into the present. Young
5 people and foreigners, however, regard it more or less as a completed historical epoch, a myth whose factual component seems to be exhausted in catch-words such as Bauhaus, the twenties, the Threepenny Opera and Marlene Dietrich.

In America recently this myth has been taken as the subject of several
10 extensive academic research projects. People are beginning to become aware of how much the Weimar Republic contributed to forming the profile of this century, particularly in America, where so many of its most important representatives found refuge after its collapse. In her standard work "Famous Emigrants", Laura Fermi, the widow of the nuclear physicist and Nobel
15 prize-winner Enrico Fermi, gives an idea of the extent and consequences of that intellectual emigration from Europe.

The collection "The Intellectual Migration", published by the Harvard University Press, contributes further to this subject. In it, authors such as Paul Lazarsfeld, T. W. Adorno and the atomic physicist Leo Szilard write about
20 the importance of exiled scientists and academics for the emergence of a modern awareness in America. In this connection mention should also be made of Hans M. Wingler's important volume on the Bauhaus, which has just been published by the Massachusetts Institute of Technology in English. It is perhaps no coincidence that 1969, the publication year of the American
25 edition, is also the year in which the two outstanding men of the Bauhaus school, Walter Gropius and Mies van der Rohe, died.

    raised and *put,* which collocate with *question. Discussed* seems to imply too full a treatment of the subject, and *dealt with* even more so. *Tackled* implies a degree of deliberateness and determination in dealing with a subject which is not suggested by *angeschnitten.*
3 **were recently published** – kürzlich ... erschienen sind: also *recently*

appeared/came out. The Present Perfect would also be possible here. *Recently* refers to a period of time in the past, but fairly close to the present. It can be perceived both as an adverb denoting solely past time, in which case it is accompanied by the Simple Past, and as an adverb with a present reference ('during the last few days/weeks up to now'), in which case it is accompanied by the Present Perfect. In this text, either interpretation seems possible. The relative clause can be replaced by a Past Participle construction *published recently in America*, which can stand either after *books* or after *heritage.*

4 **a piece of history** – ein Stück Vergangenheit: the translation *relic of the past* is inappropriate here, as it suggests something with no link to the present, whereas according to the text the Weimar Republic actually has a link to the present for its survivors.

4 **young people** – die Jugend: also *the young. Die Jugend* in the sense of 'young people' is often wrongly translated as *youth* or *the youth. Youth* as an abstract mass noun refers to the period of life when one is young, as opposed to old age. *Youth* as a concrete countable noun is often used to denote a boy or young man in the transitional stage between boyhood and manhood. *Youth* as a collective noun in the sense of 'young people' occurs virtually always specified, in phrases such as *the youth of today,* or in collocations such as *youth club, youth centre.*

5 **foreigners** – das Ausland: also *foreign countries,* although the linking of the two nouns denoting persons is probably better here.

6 **factual component** – Wirklichkeitsgehalt: also *factual constituent/element/ content.* Also possibly *connection with reality.* Not *real component,* as *real* here would imply 'true' as opposed to 'false' or 'falsely-assumed', and not, as the text suggests, 'factual' as opposed to 'fictive'.

9 **of several extensive academic research projects** – mehrfach ... umfangreicher akademischer Untersuchungen: *mehrfach* can be rendered either as directly modifying the translation of *Untersuchungen,* or in an adverbial phrase. *Several* collocates with countable nouns in the plural form. As *research* is a mass noun, **several researches* is unacceptable. Either a countable noun (for example, *research projects, enquiries*) or a partitive (*pieces of research*) must be sought. Variant: *a number of large-scale scholarly investigations.* If *mehrfach* is rendered in an adverbial phrase (e.g. *on several occasions, several times*), the problem arises of its position within the sentence, as two other adverbial phrases – *in Amerika* and *in letzter Zeit* – also have to be contained within the sentence. All three can be placed initially – *on several occasions recently in America. In America* can also be placed at the end – *extensive academic research in America.*

10 **are beginning** – beginnt: the Simple Present would be inappropriate here as it would arouse in the reader the expectation that either a general statement or some sort of habit were to be described, e. g. *people begin to think about the future whenever there is a financial crisis.* In this text, however, the author is clearly referring to a process occupying a period of time which has already started and which extends into the future.
11 **contributed** – beigetragen hat: either Simple Past, whereby the period during which the Weimar Republic made its contribution is seen to be clearly in the past, or the Present Perfect in its resultative function, whereby the contribution is felt to exist in the present.
11 **... to forming** – dazu, ... zu prägen: also *to the formation of.* Note that *to* has a prepositional function here; *to forming, to the forming of* are possible, but not *(contributed) to form,* which would imply 'in order to form'. Variants: *to moulding/shaping.*
11 **profile** – Gesicht: *face* would be possible, but seems less likely.
12 **particularly** – vor allem: also *especially, above all,* but not **before all.*
13 **found refuge** – Zuflucht fanden: also *found sanctuary/asylum.*
13 **after its collapse** – nach dem Zusammenbruch: the association between *Zusammenbruch* and *Weimarer Republik* is obvious to the German, but the English-speaker does not automatically associate the two. For this reason, *collapse* must be given a clear reference, either through the possessive pronoun *its* or as in *after it collapsed.* Variants: *after its break-up, after it broke up.*
13 **standard work** – grundlegenden Werk: *fundamental work* might be possible, but *fundamental* and *basic* would both seem more likely in structures such as *a work of fundamental/basic importance/significance/value,* and might be incorporated into the sentence as follows – *in her book "Famous Emigrants", a work of fundamental value, Laura Fermi ...*
14 **physicist** – ...physikers: not *physician,* which is used to denote a doctor who heals by drugs and medicines, as opposed to a surgeon, who heals by operating.
15 **extent** – Ausmaßen: also *size, range, dimensions.*
15 **consequences** – Tragweite: also *effects.*
16 **intellectual emigration from Europe** – Abwanderung des Geistes aus Europa: also *emigration of Europe's intellect,* whereby *intellect* is a synecdochic collective for *intellectuals.* Also *of Europe's intellectuals/intelligentsia/ intellectual elite.* Not *genius,* as this implies intellectual or creative ability which is not just high, but of an extraordinary nature.

17 **collection** – Sammelband: not *anthology*, which is a collection of pieces of a literary rather than a social or historical nature; not *miscellany*, which is a collection of heterogeneous pieces, varying in genre, style, register, and content, whereas here we have what is presumably a fairly homogeneous collection.

17 **published** – herausgegebene: not *edited*, which refers to the organization of the material to be printed, whereas *published* here refers to the actual physical production of the book by the publishing house.

18 **contributes further** – einen weiteren Beitrag ... leistet: also *makes/offers/provides a further contribution*. The sentence can also be constructed as follows: *a further contribution ... is made/offered/provided to this subject by the collection ...*

18 **such as** – wie: *like* would be inappropriate here. *Like* implies 'similar to' or 'not very different from', which in turn implies that however great the similarity, the two items linked by *like* are nevertheless different. In this sentence, the use of *like* would imply 'authors resembling Lazarsfeld, Adorno and Szilard, but not including them', which is not the meaning of the German text. The relationship between the items when linked by *such as* is that the second element is an example of the first, i. e. that Lazarsfeld, etc. are examples of the authors contributing to the collection.

---

14. Aus dem Vorwort zu einer Interpretationssammlung

Wie die Bände zur englischen Lyrik und zum Roman, so möchte auch diese Sammlung von Interpretationen keine Gattungsgeschichte ersetzen, sondern an eine Reihe bedeutender Texte heranführen und zugleich verschiedene Methoden der Drameninterpretation gegeneinanderstellen. Auch heute noch gilt, daß der Zugang zur Literatur vor allem über das einzelne Werk führt und sich nur von hierher die größeren Zusammenhänge erschließen. Die Vielfalt der aufgenommenen Dramen ließ eine eintönige Folge gleichartiger Textanalysen von vornherein nicht erwarten. Auch hatten alle Mitarbeiter freie Hand bei der Auswahl der für den jeweiligen Text angemessenen Methode und wurden dazu ermuntert, einzelne ihnen zentral erscheinende Aspekte herauszugreifen, um nicht den Eindruck einer auf Vollständigkeit bedachten „Gesamtinterpretation" zu erwecken. Der Herausgeber hofft überdies, daß

20 **importance** – Bedeutung: also *significance.*
20 **emergence** – Entstehung: also *development, rise.*
20 **of a modern awareness** – eines modernen Bewußtseins: also possibly *of modern thinking, of a modern consciousness.*
21 **mention should be made** – muß ... erwähnt werden: the sentence can also be constructed as *one should/must mention ...* or *Wingler's important volume ... should/must be mentioned.* However, if this latter construction is used, the relative clause *which was published ...* cannot follow the verb phrase as it is then too far from its antecedent *volume.*
23 **in English** – in englischer Sprache: also *in the English language.*
23 **it is no coincidence** – es ist ... kein Zufall: also *it is no accident, it is not mere chance.*
24 **the publication year** – das Erscheinungsjahr: also *the year in which the American edition appeared/was published, the year of publication of the American edition.* The sentence can also be constructed as follows: *the fact that the American edition appeared in 1969, the year when ... died, is perhaps no coincidence.*
25 **of the Bauhaus school** – des Bauhauses: also *of the Bauhaus group,* or as a modifier in *the two outstanding Bauhaus men.*

---

14. An Extract from the Introduction to a Collection of Interpretations

Like the volumes on English poetry and the novel, this collection of interpretations does not aim to replace a history of the genre, but rather to lead up to a series of important texts, and at the same time contrast various methods of dramatic analysis. Even today the thesis is still valid that access to
5 literature is gained above all via the single work of art and that only in this way can the larger relationships be explored. The variety of dramas dealt with precluded from the very start a monotonous series of similar textual analyses. Furthermore all the contributors were given a free hand in the choice of the method appropriate to the text in question, and were encouraged to select
10 single aspects which appeared to them to be of central importance, in order to avoid arousing the impression of an "all-inclusive interpretation" aimed at exhaustiveness. Moreover the editor hopes that the work has gained in

durch die Beteiligung zahlreicher jüngerer Wissenschaftler das Werk an Breite und Lebendigkeit gewonnen hat.

Die Beiträge unterschieden sich auch dadurch stark voneinander, daß sie, was den Stand der Forschung anlangt, von sehr unterschiedlichen Voraussetzungen auszugehen hatten. In einzelnen Fällen — dies gilt insbesondere für Shakespeare — wird eine Interpretation kaum völlig neue Ergebnisse bringen, sondern allenfalls die Akzente etwas anders setzen können, während von manchen anderen Dramen bisher noch so gut wie keine ausführlichen Deutungen vorlagen. Dies hängt auch mit der Auswahl zusammen, deren durchaus persönlicher Charakter gern eingestanden wird und die im einzelnen erst im Gespräch mit den Mitarbeitern festgelegt wurde. Selbstverständlich sollten die Dramatiker am stärksten vertreten sein, deren Wirkung auf das englische Theater besonders nachhaltig ist und die auch für den deutschen Leser ausgesprochenes Interesse haben. So war von Anfang an klar, daß die Zeit Shakespeares und das 20. Jahrhundert die eigentlichen Schwerpunkte bilden würden; doch innerhalb dieses Rahmens sollten auch solche Werke herangezogen werden, die selten oder nur in Liebhaberaufführungen auf der Bühne erscheinen, wenn sie nach Meinung des Interpreten bisher vernachlässigte Qualitäten besitzen oder sich an ihnen besonders aufschlußreiche literarische Zusammenhänge illustrieren lassen.

Aus: D. Mehl (Hg.), *Das englische Drama.* Düsseldorf: Bagel, 1970.

Commentary

Introduction — Vorwort: possibly *preface, foreword. Prologue* in its technical sense is usually limited to the introduction to a play, and is usually performed.
Collection — Sammlung: possibly *compilation,* but not *anthology,* which suggests that the interpretations included had previously appeared elsewhere, whereas these interpretations were commissioned for this book.
2 **does not aim** — möchte ... keine ...: variants: *is not designed, does not intend, is not intended,* or *it is not the aim/intention/design of this collection.*
2 **to replace** — ersetzen: also *to provide a substitute for.*
3 **lead up to** — an ... heranführen: also *introduce the reader to, acquaint the reader with, provide an introduction to.*
3 **contrast** — gegeneinanderstellen: both *oppose* and *confront,* while possible, suggest rather more polarity between the methods of dramatic analysis than the more neutral *contrast.*

breadth and vigour through the participation of numerous younger scholars.
The contributions also differed widely because they had to start out from
15 very different premises as regards the stage research in their field had reached.
In certain cases — and this is particularly true for Shakespeare — the
interpretation will scarcely be able to reach entirely new conclusions, but at
the most shift the emphasis somewhat, whereas in the case of several other
plays virtually no detailed studies were hitherto available. This is also
20 connected with the selection, the personal nature of which is readily
admitted, and which was only decided on in detail in discussion with the
contributors. It goes without saying that those dramatists whose influence on
the English theatre is particularly lasting and who are of special interest to the
German reader should be most strongly represented. Thus it was clear from
25 the beginning that the main stress would be on the Shakespearian age and the
20th century; but within this framework other works should be included
which are staged rarely or only in special performances, if in the opinion of
the interpreter they possess hitherto neglected qualities, or permit the
illustration of particularly instructive literary relationships.

4 **dramatic analysis** — Drameninterpretation: also *interpretation of dramas/ plays.*
4 **the thesis is still valid** — gilt: variants: *it is still true/valid, it still holds good,* possibly *it is widely accepted.*
4 **access to literature is gained** — der Zugang zur Literatur ... führt: variants: *the path to literature leads..., (it is the single work that) opens the door to literature, (the single work) is the path that leads to literature.*
5 **only in this way** — nur von hierher: also *only when seen from this viewpoint/position, when viewed from this angle.* Note that if the *only-*construction is placed initially in the clause, the following subject and verb will be inverted. The sentence can also be constructed as *the larger relationships only reveal themselves when seen from the viewpoint ...*
6 **the larger relationships** — die größeren Zusammenhänge: also *the broader contexts.*

6 **can be explored** – sich ... erschließen: also *be perceived*. The versions *begin to unfold, begin to reveal themselves* are closer to the original.
6 **dealt with** – aufgenommenen: note that *dealt with* postmodifies the noun. If *included* is used, then a variant must be sought for the following verb, here translated as *precluded*.
7 **precluded** – ließ ... nicht erwarten: also *made ... unlikely, prevented the possibility of ..., made ... impossible*. The sentence can also be constructed as: *a monotonous series of similar textual analyses was not to be expected/anticipated due to the variety ...*
7 **series** – Folge: also *sequence*.
8 **all the contributors** – alle Mitarbeiter: also *all those who contributed to this book, everyone who worked on this book, all the authors*. *Collaborator* is possible, although it seems rather out of place here, perhaps because it implies 'working together' whereas these authors worked singly on their individual interpretations, perhaps because *collaborator* or the verb *collaborate* tend to occur more frequently in the context of film-production. *Collaborator* also tends to have negative associations.
8 **were given a free hand in the choice** – hatten ... freie Hand bei der Auswahl: also *were completely at liberty as far as the selection ... was concerned*.
9 **the text in question** – den jeweiligen Text: also *the particular text*, or *the text concerned*, if *concerned* has not been used in the translation of *bei der Auswahl* (see previous item).
9 **to select** – herauszugreifen: also *to pick out/extract*, possibly *stress/emphasize/lay particular emphasis on*.
10 **which appeared to them** – ihnen ... erscheinende: also *which seemed to them, which they considered to be, which they thought to be*.
10 **in order to avoid arousing** – um nicht ... zu erwecken: also *in order not to arouse*. *Arousing* might possibly be omitted completely.
11 **all-inclusive interpretation** – Gesamtinterpretation: variants: *total/complete/comprehensive interpretation*.
11 **aimed at** – auf ... bedachten: also *intended to be, with claim to, laying a claim to*.
12 **exhaustiveness** – Vollständigkeit: also *completeness, comprehensiveness*, if their adjective forms have not already been employed to translate *Gesamt-*.
12 **moreover** – überdies: also *in addition, furthermore*.
12 **the editor** – der Herausgeber: the *editor* in this case is the person who is responsible for commissioning the various contributions, and preparing the final manuscript to be sent to the publishers, who in turn are responsible for the printing and distribution of the book. *Publisher* would be wrong in

this text. Note however that the person whose responsibility it is at the publishers to accept or reject material for publication, and supervise it during the printing process, is also referred to as *editor*.

12 **work** — Werk: also *volume, book*.
13 **breadth** — Breite: also *scope*. Although *breadth* and *width* are often synonymous in concrete use, *width* is only very rarely used in a figurative sense, and would be inappropriate here.
13 **vigour** — Lebendigkeit: also *vitality*. Nouns based on *vivid, vivacious, sprightly, lively* and *brisk* are all incongruous here as they have inappropriate connotations connected with the collocations in which they normally occur. The connotations of 'youth', 'strength' and 'energy' in *vigour* and *vitality*, on the other hand, make them appropriate here.
13 **scholars** — Wissenschaftler: also *academics*, but not *scientists*, as this is used of those who work in the natural sciences.
14 **widely** — stark: also *considerably, greatly*.
14 **they had to start out from** — sie ... auszugehen hatten: the sentence can be reconstructed as follows: *the conditions they had to start out from/their starting-points varied enormously, the conditions they had to take as their point of departure varied considerably*.
15 **as regards the stage research in their field had reached** — was den Stand der Forschung anlangt: also *as regards the stage reached by research in their field, as regards the level of previous research*. Also *as far as... was concerned, concerning..., regarding...*
17 **will scarcely be able to reach** — wird ... kaum ... bringen: *kaum* in this sentence needs to be expanded in English. Other possible translations: *can hardly be expected to reach, it can hardly be expected that (the interpretation) will reach, it is unlikely that (the interpretation) will produce*.
17 **reach conclusions** — Ergebnisse bringen: also *come to/arrive at conclusions, produce/present results/insights*.
17 **entirely** — völlig: also *totally, completely, absolutely, altogether*.
18 **shift the emphasis** — die Akzente anders setzen: also *change/alter the emphasis/stress/accents*, also *put the stress on different aspects*.
18 **in the case of several other plays** — von manchen anderen Dramen: *in the case of* has been added in order to reproduce the opposition in the German sentence — *in einzelnen Fällen ... während von anderen Dramen ...* — as the opposition is greatly reduced if *von manchen anderen Dramen ... keine ausführlichen Deutungen* is translated as *no detailed studies of several other plays*.

19 **virtually no** – so gut wie keine: if *hardly* or *scarcely* are used here, note that these adverbs already contain a negative component, and the construction is *hardly/scarcely any*.
19 **is also connected with** – hängt auch ... zusammen: also *this is also partly due to, this has to do with*.
20 **personal nature** – durchaus persönlicher Charakter: also *personal character*. *Durchaus* can be translated by *indeed (the indeed personal nature of which)*, but this is not absolutely necessary as the idea conveyed in *durchaus* is also present in *freely admitted*.
20 **is readily admitted** – gern eingestanden wird: also *is freely confessed*, or *(the personal nature of which) we freely/readily admit/confess to*.
21 **which was only decided on in detail** – die im einzelnen erst ... festgelegt wurde: also *the details of which were only decided on/settled/fixed/finalized*.
22 **it goes without saying** – selbstverständlich: also *it was beyond question, there was no question but that*.
22 **whose influence is ... lasting** – deren Wirkung ... nachhaltig ist: also *who have had a ... far-reaching effect*, although this necessarily excludes contemporary dramatists.
25 **the main stress would be on** – die eigentlichen Schwerpunkte bilden würden: also *would bear the main emphasis, would form the centres of emphasis*.
27 **are staged** – auf der Bühne erscheinen: also *are performed*, if *performance* is not used for *-aufführungen*. Also *put on stage*, but not *appear on (the) stage*, which might be applied to an actor, but not to a play.
27 **special performances** – Liebhaberaufführungen: in order to translate *Liebhaberaufführung* we need to analyze what this actually is. It is presumably the performance of a play which would not normally be in the regular repertoire of a theatre company as it does not draw the public in sufficiently large numbers. The audience might be invited, or the members of a theatre club or society. The performance might well take place in a small 'studio' theatre. The actors would probably be professional, but might under certain circumstances be amateurs, for example the members of a theatre workshop. This gives us several translation possibilities – *theatre-club performance, private performance, studio performance, workshop performance*. Each of these, however, stresses one single aspect. Students frequently translated *Liebhaber-* as *amateur*, but this is unacceptable here, as an *amateur performance* is simply a performance by non-professionals, and such amateur performances usually tend to be of well-known plays. *Amateur theatricals* is inappropriate here as it has

connotations of being not very well produced. Thus *special performances*, as the most general term, seems the best choice.
28 **permit the illustration of** — sich ... illustrieren lassen: also *allow the illustration of*, or *(if ... relationships) can be illustrated by means of them*.
29 **instructive** — aufschlußreiche: also *informative, illuminating*.

Wichtige Hilfsmittel

Die Übersicht umfaßt die wichtigsten Hilfsmittel, die jedem Benutzer der Texte zur möglichen Anschaffung für seine eigene Bibliothek empfohlen werden.

1. Einsprachige Wörterbücher

The Shorter Oxford English Dictionary on Historical Principles.
Prepared by William Little, H. W. Fowler, J. Coulson: Revised and Edited by C. T. Onions. Third Edition. Oxford: Clarendon Press, 1944, repr. 1965 (1933).
Gekürzte Ausgabe des *Oxford English Dictionary;* enthält neben vielen Autorenzitaten aus vergangenen Jahrhunderten vor allem präzise Definitionen und Angaben des Sprachbereichs in sehr stark nach Bedeutungsnuancen gegliederten Beiträgen; für zeitgenössische Termini und Bedeutungen weniger geeignet.

Oxford Advanced Learner's Dictionary of Current English.
New Edition. Ed. A. S. Hornby. Berlin: Cornelsen & Oxford University Press, 1974.
Diese völlig neu bearbeitete Ausgabe ist wichtigstes Hilfsmittel bei allen sprachpraktischen Aufgabenstellungen; die einsprachig-definierenden Erklärungen werden zumeist durch Beispiele in grammatisch repräsentativen „patterns" ergänzt; Konkreta werden vielfach durch Bilder verdeutlicht.

Collins English Learner's Dictionary. Bearbeitet von D. J. Carver, M. J. Wallace, J. Cameron. Stuttgart: Ernst Klett, 1974.
Dieses einsprachig angelegte Wörterbuch zeichnet sich vor allem durch gut verständliche Definitionen aus, die in vielen Fällen durch entsprechende Beispielsätze und durch Hinweise zum Anwendungsbereich angereichert werden. Das heutige moderne Englisch findet dabei besondere Berücksichtigung.

2. Zweisprachige Wörterbücher

Langenscheidts Enzyklopädisches Wörterbuch der Englischen und Deutschen Sprache. Herausgegeben von Otto Springer. Bd. II/1 Deutsch – Englisch A–K, 1974. Bd. II/2 Deutsch – Englisch L–Z, 1975. Berlin und München: Langenscheidt.

Hierbei handelt es sich um das gegenwärtig umfassendste deutsch-englische Wörterbuch mit über 200 000 Stichwörtern. Hervorzuheben sind die Aktualität des Wortschatzes aus den verschiedensten Lebens- und Fachbereichen und die Berücksichtigung des Britischen und des Amerikanischen Englisch.

Langenscheidts Handwörterbuch Englisch. Teil II: Deutsch – Englisch. Von Heinz Messinger. 6. Aufl. Berlin und München: Langenscheidt, 1965 (1964).

Ein umfassendes und besonders empfehlenswertes Nachschlagewerk. Gute Anordnung, präzise Übersetzung, Verwendung von leicht verständlichen Symbolen für verschiedene Sprachbereiche; sehr gegenwartsnahes Vokabular von großem Umfang; in der Einbeziehung der umgangssprachlichen Stilebene und des amerikanischen Sprachgebrauchs für alle Arten der Übersetzung geeignet.

Schöffler/Weis, Taschenwörterbuch der englischen und deutschen Sprache. Völlig neu bearbeitet von Erwin Weis und Erich Weis. Teil II Deutsch – Englisch. Stuttgart: Ernst Klett, 1967.

Enthält auf 1190 Seiten nahezu 85 000 Wörter bei einwandfreier Lesbarkeit. Damit werden die Anforderungen eines Taschenwörterbuches überdurchschnittlich gut erfüllt. Die Anzahl der Wörter, ihre systematische und übersichtliche Gliederung sowie die Auswahl des Wortmaterials machen dieses Taschenwörterbuch zu einem Hilfsmittel, das im Normalfall die Anforderungen eines Handwörterbuches erfüllt.

3. Grammatiken

R. Quirk, S. Greenbaum, G. Leech, J. Svartvik: A Grammar of Contemporary English. London: Longman, 1972.

Dieses einsprachige Nachschlagewerk ist mit Abstand die umfassendste und detaillierteste Grammatik der englischen Sprache. Dabei finden die letzten Forschungsergebnisse der modernen Linguistik Berücksichtigung. Gegenstand der Untersuchung ist die Gegenwartssprache, die durch eine Vielzahl von Beispielen veranschaulicht wird.

R. Quirk, S. Greenbaum: A University Grammar of English. London: Longman, 1974 (1973).
Eine verkürzte, handliche Ausgabe der zuvor beschriebenen Grammatik.

A. Lamprecht: Grammatik der englischen Sprache. 2. Aufl. Berlin: Cornelsen, 1972.
Hier handelt es sich um eine gründlich überarbeitete neue Auflage. Der Verfasser orientiert sich an den Grundsätzen einer funktionalen Grammatik und befolgt methodisch durchgehend das Prinzip der kontrastiven Analyse. Vorgesehen als Hochschulgrammatik für Studierende und Lehrende der englischen Sprache.

A. J. Thomson, A. V. Martinet: A Practical English Grammar. 2. Aufl. London: Oxford University Press, 1969.
Übersichtlich und klar im Aufbau; geeignet für Oberstufenarbeit und für Anfangssemester im Hochschulbereich. Nicht so detailliert wie die Lamprecht-Grammatik. Übungshefte für einzelne grammatische Gebiete liegen vor.

4. Synonymiken

Roget's Thesaurus of English Words and Phrases. Bearbeitet von J. L. Roget und S. R. Roget. Harmondsworth: Penguin Books Ltd., 1974.
Eine Sammlung von 1000 Wortfeldern, die dem Benutzer eine Vielzahl von Einzelwörtern ohne Kontext anbietet; setzt somit ein hohes Maß von passivem Wortschatz voraus. Der Benutzer kann anhand eines konventionellen Wörterbuchs die Bedeutungsunterschiede herausfinden.

Webster's New Dictionary of Synonyms. A Dictionary of Discriminated Synonyms with Antonyms and Analogues and Contrasted Words. Springfield, Mass.: Merriam, 1968.
Sehr empfehlenswertes einsprachig-definierendes Synonym-Wörterbuch, alphabetisch angeordnet mit umfangreichem synonymischen, antonymischen, analogen und kontrastierenden Wortmaterial sowie ausführlichen und präzisen Definitionen, Erörterungen der Bedeutungsnuancen (literarisches Englisch), häufig mit Beispielsätzen; zum Erwerb eines tiefer gehenden Sprachverständnisses sehr geeignet. Bei der Übersetzung schwieriger Texte erweist sich dieses Wörterbuch immer wieder als adäquates Hilfsmittel.

5. Literatur zur kontrastiven Linguistik und Theorie der Übersetzung

K.-R. Bausch: „Ausgewählte Literatur zur Kontrastiven Linguistik und zur Interferenzproblematik". Stand: Jan. 1971. In: *Babel* (Sonderdruck) 2/1971, S. 45–52.

K.-R. Bausch, J. Klegraf, W. Wilss: The Science of Translation: An Analytical Bibliography (1962–1969). Tübingen: Tübinger Beiträge zur Linguistik, 1970. Volume II 1970–1971, Tübingen 1972.

E. Burgschmidt, D. Götz: Kontrastive Linguistik. Deutsch – Englisch. Hueber Hochschulreihe Bd. 23. München: Hueber, 1974.

Der erste Teil dieses Buches geht auf die Fragen der Theorie des Sprachvergleichs, der Psycholinguistik, der allgemeinen Linguistik und des Fremdsprachenunterrichts ein, während sich der zweite Teil konkret und exemplarisch mit einigen Vergleichen befaßt. Eine Fülle weiterer Hinweise ergeben die ausführlichen bibliographischen Angaben, die sich, nach Sachgebiet geordnet, jeweils am Schluß der einzelnen Kapitel befinden.

W. Friederich: Technik des Übersetzens: Englisch und Deutsch. 2. Aufl. München: Hueber, 1972.

Eine interessante, von linguistischen Erkenntnissen ausgehende Einführung in die Problematik deutsch-englischer und englisch-deutscher Übersetzungen. Eine systematische Zusammenstellung typischer Schwierigkeiten wird durch eine Vielzahl konkreter Beispiele belegt. Auch als Handbuch zum Nachschlagen spezifischer Problemstellungen geeignet.

K. Reiß: Möglichkeiten und Grenzen der Übersetzungskritik. Kategorien und Kriterien für eine sachgerechte Beurteilung von Übersetzungen. Hueber Hochschulreihe Bd. 12. München: Hueber, 1971.

Wie der Untertitel besagt, ist es das Ziel der Autorin, objektive Kriterien und sachgerechte Kategorien für die Beurteilung von Übersetzungen aller Art zu erarbeiten und die Grenzen der Übersetzungskritik abzustecken. Die Untersuchung will ein sowohl trag- als auch ausbaufähiges methodologisches Modell darstellen, in dessen Rahmen alle Phänomene des Übersetzens eingeordnet werden können. Als Ergänzung dazu vergleiche die Rezension von J. Klegraf in IRAL Vol. XI/3 (1973), S. 279–282.

6. Weitere Hilfsmittel

A. Blass, W. Friederich: Englischer Wortschatz in Sachgruppen. 9. Aufl. München: Hueber, 1973.

Bietet eine englische Übersetzung für die in insgesamt 30 Sachgruppen angeordneten deutschen Vokabeln; für traditionelles Auswendiglernen von Vokabellisten geeignet.

W. Friederich: English Punctuation and Orthography. München: Hueber, 1965.

Ein nützliches Handbuch bei der Anfertigung von Übersetzungen. Alle wichtigen Probleme der Rechtschreibung und der Interpunktion werden hier behandelt. Die straffe Systematisierung des Aufbaus ermöglicht dem Benutzer einen relativ leichten Zugang zu speziellen Fragestellungen.

G. N. Leech: Meaning and the English Verb. London: Longman, 1971.

Dieses Buch bietet eine systematische Beschreibung der Beziehung Verbformen/Bedeutung und zeichnet sich zudem durch klare und verständliche Formulierungen aus.

A. Leonhardi: The Learner's Dictionary of English Grammar. 4. Aufl. Dortmund: Lensing, 1967.

Dieses Büchlein enthält eine Vielzahl von Beispielen, an denen exemplarisch verschiedene grammatische Phänomene dargestellt werden.

E. Werlich: Wörterbuch der Textinterpretation. 3. Aufl. Dortmund: Lensing, 1971.

Gedacht als Hilfe zur Interpretation von literarischen Werken, eignet es sich jedoch gut für Übersetzungstexte aus literaturwissenschaftlichem Bereich. Es handelt sich nicht um eine alphabetische Liste von Einzelwörtern; Wortfelder werden in ihrem sprachlichen Kontext, dem Kollokationsfeld, dargestellt.

Index

abstract subject 14
achieve 47
actually 27, 72
additional 78
additive 78
admire 22
adult 34

aesthetic 43
all 58
all the time 65
ambiguity 45, 48, 78
(see also *interpretation*)
annual 24
anthology 84, 86

appear 25
appropriateness 14, 27, 45,
   46, 49, 52, 58, 61, 65, 74
arrange 48
artistic 17, 43
as far as 71
as ... so ... 48

autobiography 47
awareness 85

at the back 25
bar 25
based on 28
bench 26
biographical 49
Black Rod 25
boast 65
bring back 70
British industry 70

characteristic of 15
charge 61
circle 37
in class 31
classical 47
coincidence 85
collection 48
collocation 14, 22, 23, 24, 25, 28, 38, 49, 54, 79
colloquial 29
comic strip 53
comma 19, 22, 60
command 58
compatibility 30
complete corpus 48
comprehension 30
connotation 17, 18, 20, 24, 52, 58, 62, 89
consequences 70, 77, 83
contemporary 32
content 44
continual 71
contradictory 52
on the contrary 16
contrast 86
contribute 83, 84
contributor 88
could 70
counter 59
crammed 25
crucial 42
cultural 32, 33

deal with 57
deceptive 18
deep, deeply 14
deliberately 29
demand 58
dependent 33

dinner 62
disregarded 43
disturbed 17
dominate 24
double adjective 32, 33, 34, 42, 43
double negative 22

each 36, 59, 76
economic 37, 64
economical 37, 64
education 36
embody 25
emerge 49
eminent 49
emotionally 34
emphasis 16, 27, 63, 75, 76
employ 16
English-speaking 52
enormous 65
entirety 17
eradicate 17
essential 36
every 36, 59, 76
evidence 71
evident 23
examined 40
exhausted 38
expansion 37
express 23
extensive 82
extinguish 61
extremely 31

face 39
fact-orientated 54
feel 69
figure 52
first to 68
foundation 36

gain 38
gaze 14
gender 37, 70
genesis 40
gradually 34
growth 37

habit of/to 60
has to 55
hidden 79
historic 23
historical 23

host 73
hothouse 20
House of Commons/Lords 24

if, as if 12, 26, 29, 60
imperfectly 30
in/on 26
indeed 49
indication 71
initial 30
in spite of,
    despite 15, 71
intellectual 17, 33, 34
intend 45, 86
intention 45, 86
interaction 32
interference 56, 65, 70, 76, 78
interpretation 21, 33, 34, 39, 42, 54, 71, 72, 76, 82, 90
introduction 86
inversion 16, 77, 87

know 45
know-how 70
knowledge 70

labour 72
lack 23
lead 25
leader 38
life 49
like 84
linguistic 28, 31, 78
listening comprehension 28
literary 55
literary form 49
long since 23
-ly 43, 55, 60, 64

many-sided 54
meaning 46
means 61
melancholy 23
merely 79
metaphor 20
methodology 78
minute 50
modern 79

narrative structure 75
nation 27, 69
nature 53